LONG DISTANCE RIDING

LONG DISTANCE RIDING

MARCY DRUMMOND

HOWELL BOOK HOUSE INC.
230 Park Avenue, New York, N.Y. 10169

Published 1987 by Howell Book House Inc.
230 Park Avenue, New York, N.Y. 10169

Library of Congress Cataloging-in-Publication Data

Drummond, Marcy.
  Long distance riding.

  Bibliography: p.
  Includes index.
  Summary: Describes the sport of endurance riding and
discusses the training and care of the horse groomed for
this purpose and the necessary equipment and training for the
rider.
  1. Endurance riding (Horsemanship) [1. Endurance riding
(Horsemanship) 2. Horsemanship] I. Title.
SF296.E5D78   1987   798.2′3   86-27301
ISBN 0-87605-861-6

Picture Credits

Line illustrations by Elaine Roberts

Typeset by Alacrity Phototypesetters, Banwell Castle,
Weston-super-Mare, Avon
Printed and bound in Great Britain

Contents

Acknowledgements

Penelope Dauster and Georg Riedler of ELDRIC for information supplied; 'Potato' Richardson for the experience of riding in the Tevis Cup Ride; Peter Favier for allowing me to ride Mr Magoo; Brian Vaughan and members of the EHPS Council, especially Ossie Hare and Stephen Humphreys; Diane Swales and the BHS LDR Group Committee, especially Alison Kent for help regarding ride organisation; riders and back-up crews everywhere who have passed on the benefit of their experience, including Pam James, Pauline Holloway, Sue Broughton, Steve and Carole Tuggey, Christine and David Hull, Joan Allen, Valerie Long, Thea Toomer-Baker, Judy Beaumont, Margaret Montgomerie, Julie Martin, Sally Scorey, Jane Welcher, Denise Passant and many more; and especially Tony Pavord, MRCVS and experienced long distance riding vet, for reading the manuscript and advising on the many technical veterinary aspects.

Introduction

What is Long Distance Riding?

The founder of the famous 100-mile Tevis Cup Ride, Wendell T. Robie, defined long distance riding in the simplest way when he said 'Let's ride – really ride!' Today, if you are looking for a new equestrian challenge, combined with a way to improve your horsemastership, long distance riding is for you.

A fuller definition, still keeping it simple, is given in the Statutes of ELD-RIC (the European Long Distance Rides Conference): 'A long distance ride is a competition where horse and rider must cover a set distance against the clock or at a set speed. The protection of the horses is an integral part of the competition and is achieved through the appropriate qualified veterinary surveillance. Rides may be of one or more days.'

To the initiated it is quite amazing how little knowledge of the sport there still is among those engaged in other horse pursuits. Ideas vary from 'It must be terribly cruel to the horse to ride all that way in one day' to 'It's mostly for middle-aged ladies who don't have the nerve to jump, isn't it?'

Many people have absolutely no idea of the capacity of the horse to excel in distance work, the sort of speeds achieved, the skill that goes into preparing a horse for a long ride, or the fitness required of the rider to undertake the challenge of a major event.

Fig 1   Signpost on the Tevis trail, California.

Brief History

Looking back into history, it is clear that man has always used horses to travel long distances, often carrying heavy burdens. Xenophon, Alexander the Great and Genghis Khan all knew the worth of the horse for travel, transport and as an instrument of war. The coming of the internal combustion engine and modern technology heralded the changing place of the horse in society and the transfer of his many abilities to use for pleasure and in sport.

Our great grandfathers would have thought nothing of walking miles to work, putting in a twelve-hour day and walking home again. Similarly, it was not particularly unusual for a horse to do all kinds of work, six days a week, for many more hours than we would expect of him today. It is still a standing joke in Ireland that a farm horse would work all week in the fields and on his day off be allowed to enjoy a full day's hunting!

The ability of the horse to do long distance work is, therefore, without question. The ability of the rider to get him fit enough to do it is another matter.

In the history of long distance riding as a sport, there are grounds for some of the mistaken ideas about it. In the 1890s and early 1900s some disastrous rides were run on the Continent in which horses died, giving rise to the bad reputation which has dogged the sport for so long. Probably the most infamous of all these was the competition between the Prussian and Austro-Hungarian cavalries in 1892, when a race without conditions was arranged between their respective capitals of Berlin and Vienna. The distance was about 400 miles, depending upon the route chosen by the individual rider. The winning horse finished in 71 hours and 27 minutes, of which 11 hours were spent resting. Within a few days this horse, and some 25 others, had died.

In 1903 the French journal *Armes et Sport* organised a ride from Paris to Deauville. The first day's 130km (80 miles) were to be completed at a speed not exceeding 10 k.p.h. (just over 6 m.p.h.). On the second day, however, riders could take the 85km (53 miles) from Rouen to Deauville at any speed they chose. Following the ride two horses died, but at least, for the first time, there had been an attempt to look after their interests.

The original American endurance rides took place as a means of testing horses for the cavalry after the First World War and from these competitive rides of the type we know today developed, beginning with the Vermont 100-mile, three-day ride in 1936.

The first British rides of note were called 'endurance races' and were run by the Arab Horse Society in the early 1920s. Their object was to 'demonstrate to the War Office the phenomenal stamina and recuperation powers of the breed, with a view to an infusion of Arab blood into the cavalry horse.' The horses involved in these rides were all under 15hh. They each carried 13 stones in weight and covered a total distance of 300 miles on five consecutive days. Veterinary inspections were imposed and the condition of the horses before and after the ride was taken into account. The sport,

Note   To convert miles to kilometres, multiply by 1·6. To convert kilometres to miles multiply by 0·62.

both in Britain and abroad, therefore has its origins firmly based on military need.

Competitive Riding in Britain

Competitive long distance riding in Britain began with what was described as a 'summer holiday on horseback', organised by Country Life Limited in 1937. There was a choice of eight routes, all starting within 100 miles radius of the finish at Eastbourne, and a maximum distance of 30 miles in any one day. There were control checkpoints and veterinary examinations and a challenge cup for the best trained horse. Those who successfully completed the ride were awarded medals. The ride was repeated in 1938, but the outbreak of war in 1939 put an end to the event.

A decade after the first Tevis Cup Ride took place in California, the first Golden Horseshoe Ride was run in Britain. At the same time rides were being established in Australia. From 1968 the Golden Horseshoe Ride was run jointly by the British Horse Society and the Arab Horse Society, until 1975 when the BHS took over sole responsibility.

In its chequered history, the Golden Horseshoe Ride has been run in different areas of the country, over different distances and at different speeds. In 1974 it moved to Exmoor where it has been run ever since, and in 1986 the total distance over the two days was increased, for the first time, from 75 to 100 miles.

Fig 2   Pam James ready to leave Michigan Bluff on the Tevis Cup Ride. In 1985 she became the third British rider to win a Tevis Buckle.

Fig 3   Riders on the 1986 Golden Horseshoe Ride, led by Liz Finney on Showgirl II and Carole Tuggey on El Askar.

International Organising Bodies

Societies to organise and regulate the sport were formed in America and Australia and, in 1979, the various European national societies formed ELDRIC. Member countries include Austria, Belgium, France, Germany, Great Britain, Holland, Italy, Portugal, Sweden, Switzerland and Norway, with the United States of America and Australia as Associate Members.

ELDRIC instituted the European Trophy in 1980; this is a competition based on a points system, where points are won at rides which must be completed in more than one country. Two British riders, Judy Beaumont with Fforest Orchid and Thea Toomer-Baker with Nimrodel, each won the Trophy twice between 1980 and 1983. Christine Hull and William were the runners-up in 1984, with Carole Tuggey and El Askar second to the German Klaus Dittrich in 1985.

In 1980 the Federation Equestre Internationale began to take an interest in the sport and gradually a set of rules was evolved whereby rides could take place under FEI conditions. In 1985 the first official European Championships took place at Rosenau, Austria, and the first official World Championships were held in 1986 in Rome. Thus the sport has now achieved officially recognised international status, along with dressage, horse trials, showjumping and driving, and the door has been opened that could lead the way to Olympic competition.

Getting Started

This is heady stuff and all very well for the seasoned rider, but what of the beginner who might be interested and wants to know more about where to start?

British Organising Bodies

In Great Britain there are two societies which organise long distance rides. These are the Endurance Horse and Pony Society of Great Britain and the British Horse Society's Long Distance Riding Group. Each organisation runs different types of ride and has its own rules. Both societies are members of ELDRIC.

The British Horse Society is affiliated to the British Equestrian Federation, which is the national body for the control of equestrian sport in Britain and is in turn recognised by the FEI. This means that only LDR Group members are allowed to represent Britain in FEI rides abroad. Many riders in fact belong to both organisations and attempts are being made to bring the two closer together.

Endurance Horse and Pony Society

The Endurance Horse and Pony Society was formed in 1973 and runs three different types of ride. These are pleasure rides, competitive trail rides and endurance rides. EHPS rules are based on the American system.

Pleasure Rides

Pleasure rides are an introduction to the sport and are also run by the LDR Group. They cover distances from 10 to 25 miles and no veterinary judging is required, although it is occasionally provided. The minimum speed for pleasure rides is usually laid down as 5 m.p.h. which is about that of an average hack in the countryside, provided you don't dawdle.

Pleasure rides are sometimes run as sponsored rides, which adds to the interest. They are usually organised in conjunction with more serious classes and follow part of the main event route, which is marked in the usual way with coloured tape or flags. There may be a tack inspection.

Pleasure rides are an ideal way of finding out if the sport appeals to you; giving you the chance to take part in an organised ride not unduly taxing to a horse not specifically trained for the job – and not taxing you too much either! Many people who don't have time for serious distance work take part in pleasure rides simply for the opportunity of seeing beautiful countryside and 'having a go' at something. Rosettes are usually presented to all who complete the course within the time.

Competitive Trail Rides

Competitive trail rides represent the next level of the sport and are the beginning of real distance riding. In the novice section (novice applies to the horses not the riders), distances range from 20 to 25 miles and for a perfect score the speed must be between 6 and 7 m.p.h. Penalty points are awarded for speeds within 1 m.p.h. of the optimum and horses are eliminated at speeds beyond these. Penalties are also awarded for pulse and respiration rates outside set parameters (with elimination if they are too high) and for injuries incurred on the ride (with elimination for lameness).

Open competitive trail rides cover distances from 25 to 60 miles at between 7 and 8 m.p.h. for a perfect score, while fast trail rides may be from 25 to 35 miles at 8 to 9 m.p.h. The same penalty and elimination rules apply. There is also a junior division for younger riders.

Endurance Rides

Competitive trail ride rules are somewhat complicated, but endurance ride rules are much simpler. The distances range from 50 miles to the present maximum of 100 miles in one day. Endurance rides are actually races, where the first rider across the line who passes the veterinary judging is the winner.

Horses must be six years old or over (seven for 100-mile one-day rides) and to qualify, horse and rider must have 40-mile competitive trail ride gradings and/or certain LDR Group ride completions or medals. The minimum average speed, excluding halts, is 7 m.p.h. for a placing and 5 m.p.h. for a completion. Veterinary inspections take place at mandatory halts and after the finish.

There are no penalty points in endurance rides, the criteria being that the horse is 'fit to be ridden'. Pulse and respiration parameters are laid down as a maximum of 60/48 thirty minutes after the finish. Higher rates, an inverted pulse/respiration rate, or lameness mean elimination.

The most important ride in the EHPS calendar is the 100-mile one-day Summer Solstice Ride, which takes place each year on the weekend nearest to the longest day. EHPS rides are run throughout the country and there is an event taking place somewhere nearly every weekend through the season. In addition, the Annual General Meeting and awards dinner takes place in November at the end of the season, and in February a training seminar is held which features some aspect of the sport and helps members prepare for the forthcoming season.

BHS Long Distance Riding Group

The BHS LDR Group has a different system of ride organisation, although pleasure rides take a similar form. In general, the LDR Group rules regarding tack and rider wear are somewhat stricter than those of the EHPS, with tack inspections always taking place at LDR Group rides.

In 1985 a new system of grading rides was introduced, with the object of requiring riders, rather than their horses, to obtain qualifications at shorter distances before attempting major rides.

There are three levels of ride – Bronze Buckle, Silver Stirrup and Gold rides.

Bronze Buckle

Bronze Buckle rides begin with a 20-mile qualifier at 6.5 m.p.h., followed by a final of 30 miles at 7 m.p.h. It is not necessary to become a member of the Group to do a Bronze Buckle qualifier, so you can see if the sport appeals to you before you commit yourself.

Silver Stirrup

The next stage is a Silver Stirrup qualifier which is run at the same speed and distance as the Bronze Buckle final. A Bronze Buckle final can count towards your Silver Stirrup qualifications, provided your horse has been registered with the Group before the ride.

You then move on to a Silver Stirrup

final of 50 miles at 7.5 m.p.h., after which you may enter major rides. These qualifications apply to the rider not the horse, so if you acquire a new mount you do not have to go through the process again. It is assumed that by that time you will have gained enough experience not to enter a horse for a major ride without sufficient training to have a reasonable chance of success.

Gold

LDR Group Gold rides take two forms. They are either endurance rides with placings, run over one or two days, or they are rides to a set standard, usually run over two or three days. The latter do not have an overall winner, but medals are awarded to those completing the ride at a specified speed without incurring veterinary penalties. Gold medals are awarded to riders with a completely clean sheet (the top specified time and no penalties), with silver and bronze medals awarded for combinations of lower speeds and/or penalties. In both types of ride, completion rosettes are awarded to everyone completing the ride within the maximum time limit.

Summary

There is much discussion as to whether it is more difficult to do a one-day ride than a two- or three-day ride. No firm conclusion can be drawn. On the one-day ride the horse has to keep going for a much longer period, while on the two- or three-day ride he can have a rest overnight. Unfortunately this also gives him an opportunity to stiffen up.

Discussion also centres on whether a

Fig 4 Veterinary inspections are an integral part of long distance rides.

one-day specialist can be equally good at rides over several days and vice versa. Again, it has yet to be proved that a horse who can do one type of ride cannot do the other; the answer probably depends on the level of management provided.

Whatever type of ride appeals to you, the one thing that is consistent is the strict attention paid to the horse's welfare. Veterinary inspections have always been a feature of modern endurance rides throughout the world, in order to dispel the bad image suffered by the sport in the early days. Alongside veterinary inspections and the help and advice which vets are always willing to give to riders, the riders' knowledge of horse care and management has reached a high standard. While we seek ever higher levels of performance, the welfare of the horse is always paramount.

Distance riding as a sport is still young, and so is constantly changing. Each year we learn more about how to improve the care of our horses and help them to perform better. This makes it a very exciting sport to be involved in and the opportunity to learn exists throughout all levels of competition.

Endurance riding is the highest level of the sport and throughout this book I shall assume that horse and rider are aiming towards endurance competition. The basic principles of endurance training are applicable to all levels of distance riding however, so the information given will be directed just as much towards the lower distance and competitive trail ride competitor.

There is always someone ready to help the newcomer; the lack of competition between riders makes distance riding a very friendly sport. Whether you are aiming for a completion on a pleasure ride or a placing on an endurance ride, your true competitors are the elements of nature and your own ability. This is the ultimate appeal of distance riding – the centuries-old challenge of conquering the unknown.

1 The Ideal Endurance Horse

Many riders thinking about taking up long distance riding will be planning to begin with horses which they already own, rather than setting out to buy a specialist for the job. They will be thinking initially in terms of shorter distance rides, rather than top level endurance competition, although later those who become 'hooked' may set out to buy or breed the potential top endurance animal.

By understanding the component parts of the supreme endurance horse, we can build up a mental picture of our ultimate goal. We can pinpoint the advantages and disadvantages of our own horse, and work out how to make the best of our present limitations.

We frequently hear that the Arab is the ideal endurance horse. This belief explains the huge number of Arab horses competing at all the lower and middle levels of the sport, even though many of them could never fulfil the ideal requirements. This raises the question: what characteristics of the breed predispose Arabs to success in endurance work and can these be developed further? If these characteristics are present in other breeds, can they be equally successful in the sport?

One of the exciting things about long distance riding at all levels is that as a young sport, there are no hard and fast rules about the right type of horse. Despite the success and popularity of the Arab, other breeds and cross-breeds have been equally successful. For example, former European Champion Nimrodel,

owned by Thea Toomer-Baker, is an unregistered home-bred mare by a Trakehner stallion out of a cob mare. This is just one of many examples of horses of mixed breeding achieving great success.

It will already be clear that there is more to finding the ideal endurance horse than simply choosing a particular breed, type or size of horse. Remember that in searching for the ideal, we are thinking of the horse who will excel at the highest level, a horse capable of winning the Summer Solstice Ride or a National Championship. Of course, winning is never guaranteed, but the horse you choose must possess all the potential for success at this level. It is therefore necessary to examine the following aspects of the horse: breeding and type, conformation, temperament and certain intrinsic qualities such as individual metabolism and hereditary soundness.

Breeding and Type

Arab

Among the natural qualities of the Arab are soundness and stamina evolved through centuries of desert life, a basic conformation enabling him to carry weight at speed for long distances and over rough ground, whilst a fine build ensures there is no excess bodyweight. Speed, courage and innate good sense were bred into Arab horses from the earliest times. Today, it is their intelli-

15

Fig 5   Thea Toomer-Baker's Nimrodel, former European Champion.

Fig 6   Janette Mann's young Arab mare, Maha – an ideal type for endurance work.

16

Fig 7 Belinda Brigg's Thoroughbred gelding, Reproach, who won the Arab Marathon in 1982.

gence and sharpness which often cause those problems put down to 'bad' or 'hot' temperament by less sympathetic and experienced owners. Arab horses also seem to have a natural ability to pace themselves, which is a great advantage in endurance work. Finally, it must be said that the Arab is still the most consistently successful breed in the sport today.

Thoroughbred

The Thoroughbred, the other 'hot-blooded' breed, owes a considerable part of his origins to the Arab. All English Thoroughbreds can trace their history back to one or more of three oriental stallions imported into England at the end of the seventeenth and beginning of the eighteenth centuries. They were the Godolphin Arabian, Byerley Turk and Darley Arabian.

In the development of the Thorough-bred the prime consideration was speed, and anyone contemplating ownership should never forget this. The natural instinct of all horses is to flee from danger. In pursuing the power of speed, the breeders of Thoroughbreds have developed a very wary temperament and lightning quick reactions to anything which the horse sees as a threat.

The term 'high couraged', which is often applied to the Thoroughbred, relates to the horse's highly developed awareness of his surroundings. This sense of awareness tends to distract the horse from his work and can manifest itself in nervousness and excitability. For this reason, the Thoroughbred requires knowledgeable and sensitive handling and management, and sympathetic riding. He is not the mount for a nervous or inexperienced rider. He is, however, a superb athlete, and well schooled and ridden will give an unsurpassable feeling

17

of lightness, power and freedom of movement. Few long-term Thoroughbred owners are content to return to less highly-bred horses.

Perhaps because he is not the easiest of horses to manage, the Thoroughbred has in the past been much less popular as a long distance horse than the Arab. However, there have been some extremely successful Thoroughbred horses and there is no reason why the right Thoroughbred cannot perform as well as the right Arab. His one disadvantage, compared to the Arab, is his willingness to 'go till he drops'. The rider must be aware of this and be responsible for pacing the horse to suit his level of fitness and the requirements of the competition. Otherwise the horse is likely to go too fast in the early stages and burn himself out before the end.

Without doubt Thoroughbreds need more careful management than other breeds to keep them healthy and sound. Inbreeding has led to soundness problems, so when buying a Thoroughbred it is wise to check his own history and his breeding history to ensure that he comes from a basically sound line. A line that has bred good steeplechasing horses is usually the best choice.

Cross-breeds

The Arab and the Thoroughbred are the two 'hot-blooded' breeds and competitive horses in all ridden spheres benefit from the presence of some Arab or, more usually, Thoroughbred blood. The Anglo Arab is a cross between the English Thoroughbred and the Arab. This cross often produces an extremely sensitive, sharp and intelligent horse of Thoroughbred type, but usually slightly smaller

than the pure Thoroughbred. In theory he should be a superb endurance horse, combining Arab soundness and stamina with Thoroughbred speed and athleticism, but because there are so few on the competitive scene, this has yet to be proved. Part-bred Arabs or Thoroughbreds (crosses with other breeds) also make good endurance riding prospects, when the cross results in a lighter-framed type of horse.

Warmbloods are horses bred with a mixture of 'hot' Arab or Thoroughbred and 'cold' draught horse blood. They are not an obvious choice for endurance work, being in general larger, heavier and slower than the ideal. However, the Trakehner, which originated in Germany

Fig 8   Christine Lewis on her Anglo-Arab, Granby Leander.

and is perhaps closer to the Thorough-bred than other warmbloods, has enjoyed some success in the sport.

In Britain we are fortunate to have several distinctive native pony breeds, which when crossed with the Arab or Thoroughbred make excellent long distance horses. The Welsh Cob and the Connemara are particularly suitable for this purpose, while pure-bred native ponies also perform well, within the limitations imposed by their scope and size.

Cob

The cob is not a breed but a type of horse, and unfortunately one which declined when 'gentlemen' gave up riding them and took to driving motor cars! Whilst they hardly present a picture of the ideal endurance horse, they should not be totally ignored, as they often make up in soundness and reliability what they lack in fire and speed. This is demonstrated by Margaret Montgomerie's Tarquin, who in 1985, at 23 years old, had completed 3,000 competitive miles with the EHPS and a total of over 5,000 competitive miles.

A problem shared by cobs and other heavily-muscled horses is an inability to cope well with heat. The large muscle masses take longer to cool, and heavier horses may become distressed when competing in hot weather.

Fig 9   Sally Scorey's Squire Tebeldi – a typical example of the tough, part-bred horse that results from crossing Arab or Thoroughbred with native blood.

Heavier Breeds

Less useful than the Cob are the bigger, heavier, hunter type of cross-breeds. These include the Cleveland Bay and Irish Draught, and anything with heavy horse blood. The endurance horse is asked to sustain high speeds over long distances, and any excess size or body-weight is a definite disadvantage. Extra size does not mean corresponding extra strength or power, and could mean greater physical weakness.

Favoured Breeds Overseas

In the United States of America, the Arab holds sway as the most popular breed for endurance riding, but Saddlebreds and Morgans are also widely used, together with Standardbreds and Quarter horses. The pure-bred Quarter horse, however, is not ideal for endurance work, as he is bred specifically for sprinting and is heavily-muscled, while the Standardbred – purpose bred for trotting races – is considered to make the ideal cross with the Arab.

British mule enthusiasts should note that mules frequently compete successfully in American and Australian endurance events. They may not be fast, but they are extremely tough, able to cope with extreme conditions and to keep going almost indefinitely.

Breeding History

There are few, if any, established lines of breeding available in Britain relating to

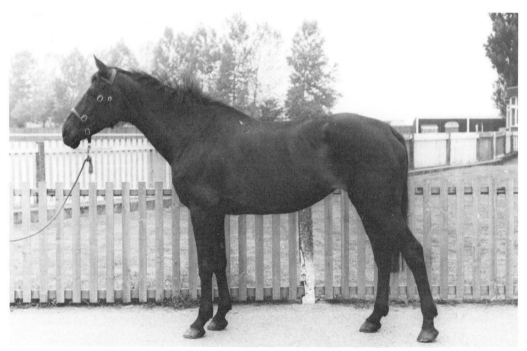

Fig 10 Jane Welcher's successful home-bred mare, Kandy Bullard.

long distance work. The best you can do is to follow the breeding of horses which have been particularly successful, and fortunately there are several Arab stallions available with proven records in the sport. Otherwise, it is a question of looking for good performance records in other spheres, in particular in National Hunt and amateur racing and eventing, where speed, stamina and soundness are important. Beware of the Thoroughbred stallion with a history of unsoundness in his racing career, and always remember that the mare plays at least as important a part as the sire in creating the potential of the resulting offspring.

Conformation

The aim of the endurance horse is to cover long distances at consistently high speeds for a lifetime's competitive career. He must perform over terrain varying from soft and springy to heavy, deep and rough. He must cope with steep ascents and descents, and vastly differing altitudes (in the United States' Tevis Cup Ride there is a variation in altitude of more than 8,000 feet over the course of the ride). He must cope with extremes of climate – heat, cold, humidity, dryness, rain and wind. He must do all this and still finish a competition in a condition assessed by the veterinary judges as 'fit to be ridden'. This is a requirement not found in any other equestrian discipline.

What kind of horse can be expected to perform consistently at this level? The answer must be a horse whose physical attributes equip him to develop his athletic ability to the highest level with the minimum of stress and strain. In other words, his mechanical make-up, or physical structure, must be designed in such a way that his job is made easier for him. In the same way that a human runner must be of a particular physical build to achieve success, the endurance horse must have the natural physical potential for the job.

Overall Picture

Conformation is the word that sums up the horse's physical make-up. There are points of conformation which are intrinsically good or bad for any horse, and there are points of conformation which are of particular importance for a horse being asked to do a particular job.

Much is to be learned by looking at the overall picture created by a horse. What we want to see is a relaxed but alert athlete, with the potential for toughness and durability. Whether or not the horse is fit does not matter at this point. What we are looking for is a strong, compact framework, with all its parts in proportion to one another and to the whole: large, strong joints; clearly defined angles with ample space for the attachment of muscles; a broad, deep front with plenty of 'heart room'; well-sprung ribs to provide room for lung expansion; clean, hard legs and well-shaped feet.

The endurance horse must not carry any unnecessary bodyweight. Therefore we are also looking for a horse who, in his natural state, is inclined towards leanness and perhaps a rather spartan appearance, but this does not mean that he should be unhealthily thin.

For the sake of his ground covering ability, the horse should have a light, possibly even fine, framework – the Arab is a typical example. However, his bone must be dense and strong. This is a concept not readily understood, as it refers to the quality of the structure of the bone itself and its ability to withstand stress – something which is not easily measured. It is recognisable, however, in specific points of conformation, in particular the length and shape of the cannon bones and the size and shape of the joints, especially the knees and hocks. The study of numerous different horses will help a rider identify what is 'good' bone and what is 'bad' bone. Basically, good bone manifests itself in short, flat cannon bones, of good depth from front to back, large, flat knees and large, well-defined hocks. Conversely, bad bone is denoted by long cannon bones which may be 'tied in' below the knee (that is, they are narrower below the knee than further down), rounded knees and weak, poorly shaped hocks.

The skeleton provides the basic structure upon which the horse is built and it should be strongly made, without weak points. The joints of the various bones are held together by ligaments and movement is effected by the contraction of muscles, attached to the bones by tendons through which they transmit their pull. These muscles, which are used for 'voluntary' movement, perform two functions. They either bend, or flex, the joint or extend the joint and return the limb to its original position.

To achieve the optimum performance with the basic structure of the horse, all his natural bodily functions, such as his digestive, circulatory, nervous and respiratory systems must be in good order. These will be considered later, in conjunction with fitness training and management. We will now look at the horse's conformation in detail.

Head and Neck

A horse uses his head and neck to help balance himself. The horse did not evolve naturally equipped to carry a rider. Man has, by selective breeding, developed different types of horse to carry riders for different purposes – everything from the warhorse carrying a heavily accoutred knight, to the racehorse carrying a slip of a jockey. In addition to development by breeding, the horse needs to be worked to develop his body to carry his rider with greater ease and efficiency. The better his natural balance therefore, the easier it is for him to carry his rider well, and his natural balance is considerably affected by the conformation of his head and neck.

A point to remember when considering the endurance horse is that the emphasis is on sustained performance over a long period of time. Whilst the lack of certain natural advantages of conformation can be compensated for by judicious training, the horse with the natural advantages will last longer.

In the dressage arena, the rider is using all his powers of concentration and trained muscular co-ordination and finesse to aid and support the horse in its work. On an endurance ride, such controlled intensity of effort would obviously be exhausting, even if it were possible. Whilst the rider must do all he can to help the horse, a great part of the skill lies in allowing the horse the freedom to perform without interference. The horse's ability to balance himself continuously, whilst carrying a rider and moving at speed, is therefore extremely important.

The head is a heavy part of the horse's anatomy, and the endurance horse's head should therefore be small, with the neck long, light and graceful, never short or thick. The eyes should be large, alert, calm and set wide apart. The ears should be alert and mobile, irrespective of size, taking in all the surrounding sounds and listening for the rider's voice. There should be plenty of hair inside the ears to keep out dust and flies; never clip inside the ears. The muzzle should be neat, with the mouth (jaws, teeth, tongue and lips) well formed, both to masticate food and accept a bit. The nostrils should be large and capable of dilation to facilitate the passage of air when the horse is moving at speed.

A clean cut face, with a fine and well-defined bone structure is a sign of quality. There should be room for the width of a fist between the cheekbones, again to allow plenty of breathing room. A well-defined jugular groove and prominent windpipe complete this aspect.

The attachment of the head to the neck should allow plenty of room for movement and flexion at the poll. The horse may not be asked to flex in endurance competition, but the ability to do so is an important part of basic schooling to improve the horse's balance and self-carriage, coupled with acceptance of the bit and the rider's aids.

The neck should flow naturally down to a well-defined wither and shoulder. There should be no build-up of muscle on the underside of the neck as this denotes an unbalanced horse who moves in a hollow outline, usually with his nose in the air. This prevents him from seeing where he is going and means he will tire easily and be uncomfortable to ride. Good muscle development along the top side of the neck, from the poll downwards and the withers upwards, is desirable; it shows that the horse is balanced and well able to support and use his head and neck efficiently. A ewe neck is to be avoided, as is a short, cresty neck, as both impair the horse's balance.

Fig 11 Outline of dressage horse, showing the compressed muscular energy required for collected movement.

Fig 12 Outline of an endurance horse, showing free, forward stretching, but still balanced movement.

Withers

Fairly prominent withers are usually seen in the higher bred, quality type of horse, whilst flat, broad withers are found in ponies and in the chunkier, cob-type horse. Well-defined withers help the saddle to sit well on the horse's back, and mean that the horse will be a comfortable ride, as good withers in the riding horse usually go with a good shoulder. Withers that are very high or narrow may cause problems with saddle fitting and may be easily rubbed by rugs, but provided you are aware of the problem there is no reason why the horse should not be suitable for endurance riding.

Shoulder

Anyone concerned with horses travelling at speed will almost certainly take the shoulder as their starting point in deciding whether or not a horse is worth buying. If the shoulder is not good, you are not looking at a good endurance prospect.

The shoulder is of such importance in assessing a horse as it gives us the clearest and most easily visible indication of the horse's overall scope for mechanically efficient and free movement. To see a good shoulder, look at any classic racehorse, chaser, top eventer or other good galloping horse.

For a top endurance prospect, a good shoulder is absolutely vital. It must be well defined, with a long slope from the withers to the point of the shoulder. The classically ideal angle is 45 degrees. A long, sloping shoulder allows plenty of room for the muscles as they develop during training.

A more upright shoulder shortens the stride, increases the effects of concussion on the whole leg and thus the risk of damage, and gives an uncomfortable ride. An upright shoulder also brings the rider's centre of gravity forward, with the girth close behind the elbow. However there may be a case for allowing a slightly more upright shoulder in the endurance horse, as will be seen when we consider the action and the conformation of the horse's feet.

Chest

The chest cavity contains the heart, lungs and gullet, so it needs to have plenty of room for these to function properly and to allow for improvement of the performance of heart and lungs by training. The chest should therefore be deep and rounded, broad but in proportion with the rest of the horse. As a guide, the girth measurement should be greater than the height of the horse for the heart and lungs to function properly during hard work. Long, well-sprung ribs add to the picture.

Back

The design of the horse equips him to carry the suspended weight of his bodily organs, rather than the compressed weight of a saddle and rider. But since the endurance horse must carry a rider for many miles, his back should be strong enough to withstand the pressure of the rider's weight.

The ideal back for the endurance horse presents us with something of a dichotomy. A short, compact back is undoubtedly stronger and able to carry weight better than a longer back. However, the endurance horse should also be able to cover the ground well at speed, and a short back reduces this capacity. On balance, the slightly longer back must give the endurance horse more scope, provided everything else is in order. But it must not be over-long, nor leading into weak loins, or poor quarters which fall away to a weak hind leg. The back should be slightly concave and follow on naturally from the withers to give a pleasing top line.

The loins, which are the least supported part of the horse's back, should be short and strong, though they will, of course, be a little longer in the longer backed horse. When the horse is fit, the loins should be well muscled and show no signs of weakness.

Abdominal Cavity

The abdominal cavity lies behind the chest cavity and is separated from it by the diaphragm. It contains much of the horse's digestive system – stomach, intestines, liver, kidneys and bladder – and the sex organs.

Thinking once again of the overall picture of the endurance horse, we should see a lean, hard, somewhat rangy creature. Do not, however, make the mistake of confusing a tight, narrow gut with a fit appearance. All the food that the horse eats has to go somewhere, and if the abdominal space is cramped, digestion is less efficient and it will be difficult to get the horse in any sort of condition to begin training, let alone to get him fit.

Quarters

The quarters should be muscular and well rounded, though in the endurance horse they may appear lighter than in horses used in other disciplines. The important thing is that any lightness relates to muscle size and not to weakness in the skeletal structure.

The croup should slope sufficiently to bring the horse's hind legs underneath him, with the tail well set on, neither too high nor too low.

Legs

An endurance horse with strong, sound legs can be forgiven a host of other faults. In our overall picture he must have 'one at each corner'. In other words, the horse must stand squarely upon his four legs with his weight equally balanced, and each foreleg and hind leg must be the mirror image of its opposite. They must be symmetrical and straight, neither turned inwards nor outwards.

In detail, the elbow should continue the scope of the shoulder for free, forward movement, being well defined and set well clear of the body. A tied in elbow greatly restricts the horse's ability to stretch forward and cover the ground.

The forearm should be strong, proportionately long and well muscled, descending into a proportionately large, flat knee. The larger the knee joint, the larger the area available to take the weight of the horse's body and absorb concussion.

The cannon bones should be short, for strength, and the same width all the way down. They may be fine, but the bone must be flat and dense. The tendons must be clean, well defined and hard.

The fetlocks should be wider than the cannon bones and well shaped, and the pastern should be neither too long, too short, too sloping nor too upright. Its angle with the ground should be the same as that of the foot.

The hind legs, on the whole, cause less problems than the forelegs. They are, however, the source of all forward movement and it is essential that in the endurance horse, they are constructed for both strength and speed. Look for a good length from the point of the hip to the hock, with a well-defined stifle. The whole structure should be supported by long, deep and well-developed thigh muscles, including a good second thigh. From behind, the thighs should look muscular, without much daylight showing between them.

The hock is a complicated joint, responsible for much of the propulsive effort. It should appear proportionately large, broad, deep, well supported from below and with a well-defined point. An endurance horse cannot afford weak hocks, yet a good hind leg is less frequently seen than a good foreleg. In America, one of the most noticeable differences between the Arab horses competing for the Tevis Cup and those seen in Britain, was the superior bone structure of the American endurance horses, especially in their hocks and hind legs.

The feet are of particular importance in the endurance horse and will be dealt with fully in a separate chapter.

Temperament

The endurance rider is going to spend a long time in the company of his horse, in training as well as in competition, so it is important that the pair get along together. Don't buy the best bred Arab or Thoroughbred you can afford, if the prospect of riding it scares you stiff! Choose a horse you feel happy with. This may seem obvious, but it is surprising how many people buy themselves problems.

Take the time and trouble to get to know and understand your horse. This is something at which many regular endurance riders excel. Horses have their own language, reactions and social rules. Learn them and much of the mystery of good old-fashioned horsemastership will become clear to you. As you come to understand why a horse behaves in a particular way, many of the so-called 'temperament problems' will disappear. You will have learned that they are nothing to worry about and how to cope with them.

Nevertheless, horses vary in temperament as much as humans, and just as certain types of temperament enable humans to excel in sport, so it is with horses. Above all, you want a horse who will enjoy the challenge of his work and will keep going when the terrain or the weather gets rough. Look for the type of horse who shows enthusiasm when you set out and who is always eager to see what lies around the next corner.

It is important to differentiate between high spirits combined with eagerness to be off at the start of a competition and a worrying, nervous disposition which wastes precious energy by fretting and refusing to settle. The latter type of horse will often refuse to eat in a strange situation; this is a great drawback when he needs all the energy he can get.

Curiosity and an awareness of all that is going on around him are good signs, but the horse must be equally aware of his rider and ready to obey orders. An over-nervous disposition may block the way to building up such a bond of communication. Anxiety is often accompanied by poor condition and poor conformation – beware of all three.

A liking for human company is a great

advantage in an endurance horse for obvious reasons, and if your horse is born with it, so much the better. However, provided the basic courage, willingness and common sense are present, the horse's character can be developed and his competition temperament improved with experience. It takes time for a horse to learn what the sport is all about and how to conserve his energy until it is needed.

Special Qualities

There are special attributes which make the difference between a good horse and a champion. In the endurance horse they are related to stamina, soundness and the will to win.

Research in the field of exercise physiology has proved that some horses are simply born with a greater capacity for endurance than others. The physical structure of their muscle fibres makes them intrinsically suited to endurance work.

Soundness is also considered to be a basically hereditary attribute, hence the warnings about breeding from horses with a history of unsoundness. If you can find a horse with that basic inbred toughness, or hardness, half the battle is won. It may be found in certain Arab lines. It is a sad fact, however, that much of the Arab's legendary toughness has been lost through indiscriminate breeding, in particular for showing rather than performance.

Hereditary soundness may also be found where an infusion of good native blood has strengthened, for example, a Thoroughbred line and been passed down through several generations. It also tends to be found in smaller, rather than

Fig 13   Bred for the sport –Pauline Holloway's foal, The Taurean, out of her successful Thoroughbred mare Clementine, by the Arab stallion, Tarim.

larger, horses.

The will to win is a less scientific concept. Suffice to say that in any equestrian sport there are heroes – horses who love adulation and applause, who perform amazing feats, break records and go down in history. Endurance riding as a sport is only beginning to produce its own great horses.

Assessing Your Horse

Every cherished equine is a star to its owner – which is why, if you are not sure about your own eye for a horse, you should ask someone with a more objective point of view, perhaps an experienced endurance rider, to help you assess the potential of your horse for endurance

27

or competitive trail riding.

The horse described earlier in this chapter is the epitome of top level endurance riding excellence, but the chances are that the type of horse most newcomers to the sport will want to begin with is the basic, good all-rounder, found all over the country at riding club events. He isn't going to win any championships, but given the right training and aimed at the right events, he will take you into the middle levels of the sport. In a couple of seasons you could be thinking in terms of Silver Stirrup level with the BHS Long Distance Riding Group, or 40-mile competitive trail rides with the Endurance Horse and Pony Society. On the way you will have a lot of fun and learn more about your horse (and possibly yourself) than you ever dreamed possible.

To assess your horse's potential and decide where to aim him, first, with the help of your unprejudiced eye, make a list of both his good and his bad points. Next,

decide how to capitalise on his good points and minimise the effect of his bad points. For example, if your horse has a rather upright shoulder and a short back, you can concentrate on teaching him to carry himself well in a balanced outline on a long rein, and then to extend as well as he can, maintaining a balanced rhythm. He will then be better able to cover the ground than if he were allowed to follow his natural inclination to a short, hurried stride. In fact, the key to minimising most problems, other than glaringly bad conformation faults, lies in improving the horse's balance, a subject which will be more fully dealt with later.

The days when virtually any horse and rider could tackle the Golden Horseshoe Ride with a good chance of success, are past. However, there is no reason why the average riding horse should not compete in long distance riding, at a level equivalent to that which it enjoys in showjumping, horse trials and dressage.

2 Daily Care and Stable Management

There are many good books available on the subject of basic stable management (*see* bibliography) and this chapter will not go into detail on the traditional principles of horsekeeping. What we shall look at are aspects of stable management which specifically affect the endurance horse and ways in which management can be adapted to meet his special needs. Bearing in mind that endurance riding is an amateur sport and many riders have full-time jobs or other commitments, we shall consider how the time needed to look after the endurance horse can be reduced without adversely affecting his welfare and performance.

Basic Routine

The first thing to consider is the basis of your horse's management routine. Is he to be stabled full time, part of the time, or kept out? In conjunction with this, is the horse being used for any other purpose and, if so, to what extent and during which seasons of the year? When does he need to be kept up and fit and when can he be let down and rested?

Rest and Relaxation

The long distance riding season runs from early March to late October, which means that most serious endurance horses have their holiday in November and December, being brought up again in January to start training for the new season. If, however, you want to hunt your horse in the winter, the situation becomes more complicated. Do you give your horse a break at the end of the summer and miss the later rides so that you can bring him up again for autumn hunting, or do you start your distance work later in the season? Whatever you decide, the endurance horse needs a complete break at some time during the year. If he is competing regularly during the season, his fitness level will be kept up, ideally peaking before each major ride. The overworked horse, just like the overworked human, becomes sour and stale. He needs a rest to allow his body to relax and recover from the stresses and strains of competition.

Many endurance horses are never given the opportunity to do anything but distance work, a combination of competitions and training rides and nothing much else. This is a pity, because a good distance horse with an outgoing nature will have the scope for other things, and variety will keep him alert and interested. Suitable alternatives may include hunter trialling, showjumping, hunting, dressage or perhaps some novice eventing, depending upon the horse's capabilities and the rider's interest, ability, time and facilities. Yet another training ride round a familiar and well-worn route, certainly adds little sparkle to the life of either horse or rider. Belonging to the local riding club is a good way to become involved in other activities at reasonably low cost.

Stabling

Whether you keep your horse stabled part or all of the time will depend upon the facilities you have available. If you have your own land, he will be able to go out more than if he is kept at livery and has to share available pasture with other horses. There is no reason why a calm, equable horse cannot be kept stabled more or less full time, in accordance with the traditional principles of keeping stabled hunters, jumpers and show horses. Many horses do live in almost permanently, with no apparent ill effects. Of course, even then they should be turned out on their rest days and, ideally, for a couple of hours after exercise each day. However, there is, as we shall see, a case

for turning out the endurance horse for longer periods than might apply to the hunter or showjumper.

Horses are turned out to grass for three main reasons – to graze, to stretch their legs and exercise themselves and to relax (and undoubtedly to roll!). Conversely, horses are kept stabled for ease of management, to prevent them from over-grazing and getting 'grass bellies', for warmth and protection from the weather in winter and for protection from flies in summer.

As a basic principle, the combined system of management is ideal. During the winter the horse goes out during the day and comes in at night. In summer it is the other way round, with the horse going out to graze at night and coming in during the day. British weather can, of course, make a nonsense of the routine – snow in April, a heatwave in November – and you must make whatever allowances are necessary.

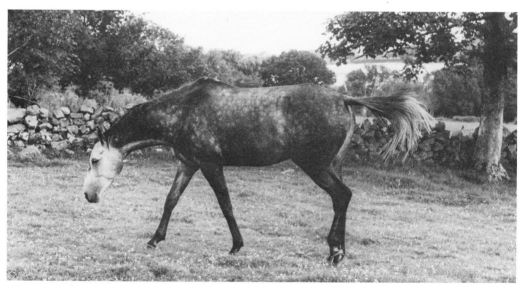

Fig 14   A chance to relax.

Letting Down
and Bringing Up from Grass

When the endurance horse has his holiday, which we will assume would be during November and December, he should be turned out all day. If he is a Thoroughbred or Arab, or has a fair amount of these breeds in him, he will need a New Zealand rug to keep out the wind and rain. (Remember, Arabs are renowned for their toughness, but they originate from hot countries where they do not have to cope with cold, wet weather, and they are thin skinned, with fine coats, so need some protection.) If the horse is a hardier type, perhaps with a good deal of native pony blood, he might well stay out all night too and, if inclined to woolliness, may not need a rug.

When the horse is brought up for training, as in any discipline, the change from no work to work must be gradual, and so must all the other changes – hours spent in the stable, feed, grooming (you will probably want to clip) and changing rugs.

The working endurance horse spends a considerable amount of time under saddle. Just before a ride and during a competition, the activity becomes more intense and the stress of work is prolonged. Horses in general much prefer to be outdoors than shut up in a stable and can relax more completely when they are turned out. Many hot-blooded horses have difficulty in relaxing, but tension or anxiety after an endurance competition can hamper the horse's ability to recover and pass the vetting. Anything a rider can do to improve his horse's general state of mental well-being will help the horse's performance in competition. It pays to turn your endurance horse out as much as you can, only drawing the line at excessive grazing and making sure that the horse does not have a belly full of grass (or any other bulk food for that matter) at the start of a competition.

Field Safety

One of the risks of turning out a horse is that you may not immediately notice any injury or accident, so a twice daily inspection at close quarters, not from the field gate, is essential. Try to make the field as accident proof as the stable. Keep fences strong and secure, with any wire well strained. Don't leave any sharp objects – fencing posts, sharp corners on drinking troughs, sheets of galvanised iron – where they can do any damage.

Keep drinking water supplies clean, fresh and free from pollution or stagnation, and make sure that any streams are deep enough so that the horse does not suck up sand when he drinks, which can cause colic. The fields must have some kind of shelter, be it a purpose-made field shelter or a thick hedge on the windward side.

Small fields rapidly become horse sick, so careful pasture maintenance is required. Good ways of maintaining healthy grassland include: resting the pasture; harrowing and fertilising when appropriate; and grazing by other animals, such as sheep or cattle, who will eat the grass the horses reject and who do not carry horse parasites. Check that there are no poisonous plants, and if there are, deal with them by pulling up and removing from the field before turning the horse out on to the pasture.

Managing the Temperament

Horses are gregarious animals with a herding instinct and a strong sense of society. If you can provide your horse with a compatible companion or two so much the better, but another horse in an adjoining field, or even some cattle, are preferable to no company at all.

The type of horse which makes a good endurance horse – sociable and interested in his surroundings – will quickly become bored without company, whether he is stabled or out in a field. Boredom is the beginning of mental and temperamental problems, which in turn lead to a less healthy horse and poorer performance.

A bored horse will become more excitable when turned out, with the possibility of injuring himself or his companions. He will be more boisterous and difficult to manage in the stable, probably showing signs of ill-temper, biting or kicking out, and he will probably develop stable vices which, once learned, are very difficult to cure. These include crib biting, wind sucking and weaving.

Stable Vices

Crib biting involves the horse catching hold of any convenient edge between his teeth, sucking in air through his mouth and swallowing it. The results are indigestion and poor condition. Wind sucking may develop out of crib biting. The

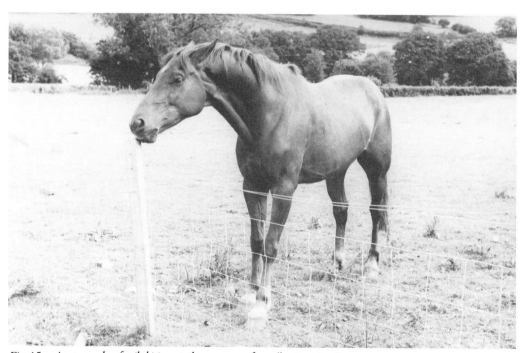

Fig 15 An example of crib biting at the moment of swallowing air, the action being accompanied by a loud grunt.

horse arches his neck and swallows air and the result is the same. Weaving describes the habit of a horse who stands with his head over the stable door, swinging his head and neck from side to side and perhaps shifting from one forefoot to the other.

Means of stopping horses from indulging in these so-called 'vices' include creosoting woodwork in the stable to stop crib biting, fitting a 'cribbing' strap which presses on the horse's throat if he tries to wind suck and fitting an anti-weaving grille over the stable door. However, these devices, though they may reduce or prevent the activity, are not cures and don't solve the problem of an unhappy horse.

It is now believed that the indulgence in these habits may induce the production of endorphins, the recently discovered natural pain-killers produced by the body. This would provide a logical reason why tense, anxious or frustrated horses start these habits, which are not necessarily copied from other horses.

The cure is to prevent boredom and change the horse's outlook on life, so that he becomes more relaxed and happy. More work, more social activity going on around him, and more time out in the field with company should provide the solution.

Stable Environment

The reason for bringing your horse into the stable is to watch him more closely and to make his management easier and more efficient when he is in training. To make your training programme effective, it is essential to keep your horse as healthy and in as good a condition as possible. This means paying close attention to his stable environment.

The stable must be spacious, with plenty of room for the horse to turn round and lie down. It must be airy and well ventilated, but also free from draughts. It must drain efficiently to prevent the horse standing on wet bedding and to allow the unpleasant ammonia fumes from the urine to escape. It should be kept as clean as possible, tidy and safe, with no sharp edges to mangers or unprotected glass windows.

Dust – the Enemy

One of the most important aspects of training any horse for fast work is that he must be clear in his wind; this is where careful stable management can make or mar the endurance horse's chances of success. Dust is probably the greatest enemy of the stabled performance horse. Recent research shows that it is the moulds present in hay and bedding which are particularly harmful and cause the disease known as COPD (chronic obstructive pulmonary disease). The disease is reversible however, and if you remove the cause in time, the symptoms will disappear. Not all horses are susceptible enough to the effect of these moulds to start coughing, but even apparently healthy horses, kept in a dusty environment, suffer a degree of reduced performance.

You should, therefore, create an environment that is as dust-free as possible for your horse. The first criteria is that the stable itself should be well ventilated, so that any dust in the air is dispersed quickly. Secondly, the food and bedding provided should be dust-free. The lengths which you go to in this respect depend largely upon the susceptibility of your horse to dust. Less sensitised horses may work perfectly well on good quality straw bedding and well-soaked, good quality hay. It may be a nuisance, but as a preventative measure it is a good idea to soak thoroughly all hay fed to competing horses.

Horses more sensitive to the moulds in hay and straw need stronger measures taken to keep their respiratory systems clear. If hay is fed, it is essential that it is well soaked first – really soaked, not just damped down. However, it may be more convenient, or even necessary in chronic cases, to feed one of the treated or ensiled hays or grasses, such as Hygrass or HorseHage, which are now easily available from feed merchants and are completely dust-free. However, they do

present the problem that they must be fed in less bulky quantities than hay, so are consumed more quickly, leaving the horse with nothing to keep him occupied during the hours he is standing in the stable. Other ploys can be introduced – feeding less but more often from a smaller-meshed net, or hanging a turnip or other suitable root fodder in the box for him to nibble.

Dust-free food is a waste of time if the horse eats it standing on a bed of dusty straw. Even good quality straw tends to be dusty, so an alternative bedding is preferable. One of the most popular is shavings, which can be bought pre-packed or loose from timber yards. Beware of the latter if you want to create a truly dust-free environment, as they may be full of fine sawdust (and may also

Fig 16 Stabled for ease of management, but the stable environment must be healthy.

contain nails or other potentially dangerous objects). You can buy pre-packed shavings which are guaranteed dust-free.

Other alternatives are shredded paper or moss peat, both of which break down into useful compost. Your choice of dust-free bedding depends upon availability and your personal preference – the important thing is to avoid dusty straw.

Finally, it is no good trying to create a dust-free environment for one horse if he is stabled next door to others being managed on traditional hay and straw. He may even be downwind of, or adjacent to, a hay and straw store. Isolate the horse, or create a dust-free environment for all.

Daily Routine

Your stable routine should follow the basic rules of stable management as regards watering, feeding, mucking out, grooming and exercise, adapted to fit in with your personal daily commitments and schedule and the training programme of your horse.

A brief look at a typical day early in the season will give an idea of the amount of time required to look after the horse and the essential points of management.

Most long distance riders have jobs to do or families to look after, so actually riding the horse has to be fitted in at either the beginning or end of the day (or for those with children at school perhaps in the early afternoon). Early rising, then, is going to be essential.

Morning Routine

Early in the season the horse will almost certainly be kept in at night and turned out during the day, so the first job will be to water him (if he does not have a constant supply in the stable) and, if you are not going to ride him first thing, to feed him. Ideally, your horse should have three or four small feeds during the day, rather than two larger ones. If you cannot attend your horse at midday, give a feed first thing, another when you get home from work, and a third last thing at night.

Grooming

Whether you muck out and groom before you feed is up to you, but most horses are hungry for their breakfasts and the job is easier if you feed first.

Night rugs should come off and the horse should be checked over before his turnout rug is put on. The long distance horse's feet must be well cared for, so pick them out. Serious grooming is best left till after exercise, but give the horse a quick brush over before turning him out if you have time. Otherwise skip it till later; he will probably come in covered with mud anyway.

If you are exercising first thing, a quick brush over, making sure his head, saddle and girth areas are clean, is enough before you saddle up. When you come back from your ride, give him as thorough a grooming as you have time for. 'Strapping' (a thorough grooming) improves muscle tone and the condition of a horse's coat. It also removes all the scurf and dirt from the skin. However, a word of warning: early in the season when the weather is cold, a horse needs the natural oils in his coat to keep warm. A little dirt does no harm either, so don't attack him too fiercely with the body brush until he becomes fitter, and you are building up to your first serious competition. Later,

35

when the horse is really fit, he will probably become ticklish and too much grooming will irritate him, so moderate the amount of grooming to suit the circumstances – don't just go by the book. Be careful how you use your grooming brushes. Be brisk, thorough, but gentle. Too much hearty pressure will also annoy the horse and cause him to take a dislike to grooming.

Evening Routine

If you are exercising in the evening, you should obviously ride before feeding as you won't get the best performance from your horse if he is trying to work and digest his dinner at the same time. Horses need at least an hour to digest a feed before being ridden.

When you arrive home from work, bring your horse in and, as you clean him up, check him over carefully for any lumps, bumps or cuts he may have sustained in the field. Pay special attention to his legs and feet. If you exercise your horse in the evening, go for your ride now and when you return your horse can cool off and relax while you groom him, put down his bed (if you haven't already done so) and prepare his feed. Don't feed him until he has had a chance to relax after his exercise – he will be tempted to bolt his food, his digestive system won't function properly and he will get indigestion, or pass the food through his system undigested.

Rug him up, see that his water buckets are filled and leave him with a haynet until you check on him again last thing at night and give him his final feed and haynet.

Other Aspects of Management

When to Clip

Whether or not to clip poses a problem when a horse is being turned out all day in cold weather and given a fair amount of exercise. The best compromise is to give the horse a racehorse clip, a trace clip or even a blanket clip in January, and by mid-March he will probably have his summer coat coming through. If your horse has been working during the early winter, he will already be clipped out by the time you start your long distance training programme.

Saving Time

If you need to save time, you can do so in the following ways without detriment to the horse. Firstly, cut down on grooming time – a silken, flowing mane and tail won't make a jot of difference to your horse's performance. Secondly, minimise mucking out – have your muckheap close to the stable and, providing your stable is well drained, try the deep litter method of bedding. Thirdly, cut down on tack cleaning – give your tack a thorough clean once a week, taking it to pieces so you can also oil it if necessary. On the other days, leave it assembled and just wipe off mud and sweat before rubbing it over with a damp, saddle soaped sponge. Always rinse the bit under a tap to remove saliva, chewed grass and hay, and dry it to prevent rust spots, although the best bits nowadays are made from stainless steel.

Coping with the Climate

In producing a horse for endurance, or any other form of long distance work, remember that he will have to compete in whatever conditions happen to prevail on the day. This may mean anything from rain, hail or even snow, to blazing sun and temperatures around 80 or 90 degrees Fahrenheit. A horse should not be so mollycoddled that he turns tail at the first sign of bad weather. Horses unaccustomed to rain and wind hate being out in it and won't give of their best, while horses to whom bad weather is a regular and common event can cope with severe conditions more philosophically.

This is another argument for turning out your horse whenever possible, and not rushing to bring him in, like the washing, at the first sign of rain. Provided he is well fed, healthy, and rugged in winter to protect him from freezing winds and rain on his back, being out won't harm him and will make him hardier and better able to do his job. Turn a couple of horses out on a snowy day and watch them. The chances are they will roll in the snow and gallop round the field with their tails in the air having as much fun as school children playing snowballs and exercising themselves at the same time. The alternative is standing in the stable, with the cold weather slowing down the circulation, then being taken for a potentially dangerous walk on slippery roads.

In Britain, coping with hot weather is a greater problem when a horse has not had time to become acclimatised to a sudden heatwave before a competition, and this is a problem we shall look at in greater detail later.

Boots and Bandages

Finally, on the subject of toughness, the endurance horse will compete without boots and bandages, unlike the show-jumper or eventer. This is because on rugged terrain, boots and bandages are likely to create more problems than they solve, and not because of any misplaced sense of machismo. Grit or gravel inside a boot for 20 miles can cause a nasty sore, with resultant penalties on some rides, so most riders prefer not to use them. This means that the endurance horse's legs need to be hard and strong, sound and straight, to do their work without protection.

There are some occasions, however, when protective boots or bandages are useful. When a horse first comes up from grass, before his legs have hardened off, he is less supple and more likely to be clumsy and knock into himself. At this time, a little support and protection is a good preventative measure.

The same precautions apply whenever you are schooling your horse, or involved in a different activity, particularly jumping. Remember, you are aiming to produce fitness, coupled with strength and endurance, and while the horse should not be wrapped in cotton wool, neither should he be exposed to careless and unnecessary risks.

3 Nutrition and Feeding

Assessing the Diet

Nutrition is probably the subject which prompts more questions from riders than any other. Where experience is lacking, most problems can be read up or muddled through, but the principles of equine nutrition have become sufficiently cloaked in scientific mystery to worry horse owners more than is necessary.

Obviously there are basic rules which should not be broken; if you can get your horse's diet exactly right, his performance and well-being will improve. The difficulty is – how do you know if the diet is right?

Much is written about providing a 'balanced' diet which also takes account of the type of horse and his workload. But let us take a look at exactly what food does for the horse and what we are trying to achieve by feeding it.

What does food do? Firstly, food maintains the natural bodily health of the horse. It provides material for the repair of cells, maintains the essential bodily functions and generates the energy necessary to keep the horse warm in its surroundings. This is food at a 'maintenance' level.

Secondly, food provides the material necessary for further physical development. It builds up the horse's muscles and improves the performance of the body systems.

Thirdly, food provides the energy required for work. It is obvious, therefore, that the working horse requires more food than a resting horse, and perhaps a different type of food.

Essential Nutrients

There are five groups of nutrients essential to the healthy horse. They are water, proteins, carbohydrates, fats, and minerals and vitamins.

Water

The largest material constituent of the horse's body is water and it is essential for the maintenance of all the main bodily functions. Water is lost when the working horse gets rid of extra body heat by sweating, in the faeces and in the urine. The horse, therefore, must have ready access to a sufficient supply of fresh, clean water. Whereas in other disciplines horses are not encouraged to drink while working, the long hours of an endurance ride mean that a horse which does not drink can become seriously dehydrated. It is good practice (and essential for endurance competitions) to stop and encourage your horse to drink from suitable supplies encountered during exercise.

There are two occasions when water should not be given freely: immediately following a meal and immediately before fast work. A horse which has become dehydrated should be offered limited amounts of water at frequent intervals, so that the system can be restored to normal gradually.

When water is lost through sweating, essential mineral salts are also lost. When a horse has been working very hard, or has become dehydrated, these salts need to be replaced for a full recovery. This can be achieved quite quickly by offering the horse water with added electrolytes. In general, a horse will only drink water containing electrolytes when he really needs them, so plain water should always be offered as well as the electrolyte drink. Electrolytes are available in various proprietary forms, either as powders or as a concentrated liquid.

Proteins

Proteins are the tissue-repairing and body-building nutrients. Most adult horses require considerably less protein than many food manufacturers would have us believe. About eight per cent is all that is required in the diet of the average adult horse, slightly more for youngstock, pregnant and lactating mares and horses recovering from injury or illness.

Proteins are made up of various amino acids, some of which can be manufactured within the horse's body, while others, known as essential amino acids, must be obtained from the horse's food. One of the more important of these is lysine, which may be lacking in a cereal-based diet. Lysine is essential for growth and tissue development, and is often included (sometimes with methionine, another essential amino acid) in proprietary food supplements. A supplement containing lysine may be useful when a traditional grain-based diet is fed to a young, developing horse who is starting work for the first time, or to an older horse who has been off work due to injury or illness.

Fig 17   A watering stop during the Golden Horseshoe Ride on Exmoor.

However, the general principle of feeding a high protein diet to working horses has little value. Proteins not utilised by the body for growth or tissue repair are converted to produce energy (which can be more cheaply and efficiently produced in other ways) or stored as fat.

Carbohydrates

Carbohydrates are the basic energy producing nutrients. They also help in the digestion of other foods. There are three types of carbohydrates: sugars, starches and fibre. Sugars and starches are both converted to glucose for immediately available energy, or stored as fat until needed, while fibre plays an even more important part in the diet of the horse than it does in the diet of the healthy human.

Fibre is obtained from the stalky parts of grass and hay and its main purpose in the diet is not to produce energy, because the horse is unable to digest most of it, but to provide the bulk which assists other food to pass through the horse's digestive system.

Fats

Fats provide a more concentrated form of energy than that produced by carbohydrates. Recent research indicates that endurance horses benefit from increased levels of unsaturated fats in their diets. This can be given as part of a proprietary high performance ration or in the form of vegetable oil added to the feed. However, the horse's ability to utilise fats stored in the body, or fed on a daily basis, improves with training, so a high fat diet will only make an appreciable difference to the performance of a hard working horse.

Fats have a higher density of energy than carbohydrates, so may be a useful addition to the diet of a horse in hard work who refuses to eat sufficient grain to keep up his condition and performance level. It is also claimed that partly replacing carbohydrates with fats in the diet reduces the likelihood of problems such as azoturia, laminitis and overexcitable behaviour.

Minerals and Vitamins

Minerals and vitamins are essential for growth, repair of body tissues and the healthy functioning of the bodily systems. They are required only in minute amounts and in an ideal world we would not need to supplement the horse's diet with vitamins and minerals at all: the grass would all be permanent pasture with a good mixture of plants and herbs, the hay would always be made in fine weather in June, and the oats would always be plump and wholesome. Unfortunately this ideal situation does not exist. Pasture is often ley, with a limited variety of plants; soil in some areas is deficient in certain minerals; it rains during haymaking and delays or spoils the harvest; and however good your intentions, the grain you buy is what you can get, not what you would like.

Supplements

Horses in light work don't usually need food supplementation. It is when you start to ask higher performance levels from your horse that you need to ensure against deficiencies. If your horse has regular access to good permanent pasture, he is less likely to suffer from vitamin and mineral deficiencies.

Unless specific symptoms are present, enabling a veterinary surgeon to diagnose a particular deficiency, it is practically impossible for the horse owner to know which minerals and vitamins, if any, are lacking in the horse's diet. The horse will appear quite normal in himself and able to carry out his workload without too much trouble. It is therefore a good basic policy to add a broad spectrum vitamin and mineral supplement to a traditional grain diet. The owner will usually then notice increased liveliness and overall well-being. The coat may develop more shine and the horse appear generally fitter and stronger.

Supplements must not be added to compound feeds without first checking whether the feed already contains added vitamins and minerals. Most do, and adding more could have a toxic effect, or will be, at best, a waste of money.

Vitamin and Mineral Requirements

You should be aware of several points regarding vitamin and mineral requirements, when balancing your endurance horse's ration.

Calcium is essential for the healthy development and strength of the horse's bones. It is found in grass and good hay, but cereals are deficient in calcium. Phosphorus is also essential for bone development, but the ratio of calcium to phosphorus in the horse's diet should be between 1:1 and 2:1. Cereals, especially bran, are high in phosphorus. Therefore a hardworking horse on a high level of cereals requires a correctly balanced calcium/phosphorus supplement to maintain healthy bones. It is available

from your veterinary surgeon or in a proprietary form such as limestone flour.

Vitamin D is required to help the horse's body absorb calcium and phosphorus. Vitamin D is mainly produced by the action of sunlight on the horse's skin, so a horse who is seldom turned out may need extra vitamin D. This requirement can be resolved by the use of a broad spectrum supplement.

Vitamin E is needed for healthy muscle function and thus for stamina and sustained high performance. It is also said to have a calming effect upon nervous temperaments. Azoturia (tying up) may sometimes be associated with a lack of vitamin E in the diet. However, high levels are present in fresh foods and cereals. For vitamin E to be utilised efficiently, selenium is required and in some areas there may be little selenium in the soil. Any deficiency of selenium in the horse can be identified by a simple blood test and corrected accordingly.

Where polyunsaturated fatty acids are present in the diet, such as in a high fat diet, less vitamin E is absorbed by the horse. A horse on such a diet may benefit from a vitamin E or vitamin E and selenium supplement, if he is not obtaining enough from other sources.

However, remember that vitamins and minerals interact with each other in many complex ways, so guessing at what is needed and settling on one or two nutrients in isolation may well do little good and more harm. Remember too that many vitamins and trace elements are toxic if overfed, so do not feed them ad lib as a matter of course. The time to supplement, other than giving the recommended amount of a broad spectrum supplement, plus a balanced calcium/phosphorus additive, is when a problem has been identified.

The horse's need for salt is often underestimated; about one tablespoon per day, added to the feed, is right for horses in hard work who are likely to sweat a great deal both working and when travelling to competitions. Don't forget the golden rule of giving your horse free access to drinking water.

Sources of Nutrients

Having looked at the essential nutrients required by the horse, we can now look at the types of food in which they are found, and how these may be combined to provide a balanced diet, in accordance with the work the horse is expected to do.

Natural Food

Grasses, together with other plants and herbs, form the basic maintenance ration for the horse in the wild. They provide, with water, all the essential nutrients. The condition of the horse relying upon natural vegetation waxes and wanes according to the time of year and the state of growth of the nutrient plants.

To produce the results we want from the domesticated, working and competing horse, we build upon this basic diet to obtain improved condition, plus greater strength and energy output when required. These results are achieved by feeding higher quality, body-building protein, considerably increased levels of high energy carbohydrates and some fats, plus the correct balance of vitamins, minerals and trace elements.

The Digestive System

The horse's digestive system is so designed that to keep it functioning properly, a relatively large volume of fibre must be consumed. Fibre is in fact carbohydrate, some of which can be digested and assimilated, but the majority of which passes through the digestive system and is excreted as dung.

The purpose of the digestive system is to consume food, convert it into a form in which it can be absorbed by the body and to excrete waste products. Digestion takes place in the alimentary canal, which runs the length of the body, and comprises the mouth, throat, gullet, stomach, small intestine and large intestine. The horse has a small stomach, but a considerable length of intestines, where much of the digestive process takes place. The process is continuous and this is why it is important to emulate the horse's natural grazing pattern by feeding small amounts frequently, not just giving two large meals a day.

Bulk Food

The fibre, or bulk food, comes from grass and hay stalks, bran, cereal husks, sugar-beet pulp and other less important sources. Proteins are available in grass (especially in spring and early summer), hay (especially well-made hay and to a greater extent in treated or ensiled hay), lucerne, clover, grass meal, oats, barley, bran, peas, beans, boiled linseed, milk and soyabean meal.

The main energy producing carbohydrates (sugars and starches) are found in cereals, succulents (such as root vegetables and apples), sugar-beet pulp, molasses, peas and beans. Compound feeds, such as coarse mixes and horse and pony nuts, contain a balanced blend of all the essential nutrients and are designed as total concentrate replacement feeds.

Thus, we feed 'bulk' for a healthy digestion and general maintenance ration, and 'concentrates' for extra condition and energy.

Teeth

The digestive process starts with the teeth, which masticate the food, beginning the task of breaking it down before it reaches the stomach. The horse's teeth continue to grow throughout his life, growth matching the wear occasioned by mastication of food. The horse, like the human, has two sets of teeth, temporary and permanent, during his life.

At the front of the mouth are the incisors, the biting and tearing teeth used for biting off grass (and sometimes as a weapon, as every rider knows!). Further back are the molars, or grinding teeth, six on each side of both jaws in the adult horse.

The horse's upper jaw is wider than the lower jaw and the constant mastication of food means that the inner edges of the upper teeth and the outer edges of the lower teeth become worn away, leaving sharp edges on their opposite sides, which may cut the cheek and tongue. The discomfort can prevent the efficient mastication of food and may lead to 'quidding' or spitting it out, with resultant digestive problems and poor condition. Bitting problems, and a reluctance to accept the bit may also ensue. The teeth should be checked twice a year by the veterinary surgeon or horse dentist, and rasped, if necessary, to smooth away the sharp edges.

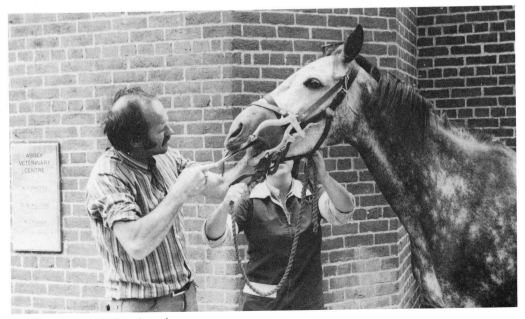

Fig 18 Rasping the horse's teeth.

Quantity of Food

Any number of books or 'experts' will advise a different quantity of food for your horse. Various complex equations have been worked out to tell you exactly how much a certain sized horse doing a certain amount of work should receive. Most of these calculations are based upon the traditional methods of feeding hunters and are not necessarily valid for the endurance horse. From recent research it has become evident that far more problems result from overfeeding than underfeeding. Quality is of more significance than quantity, and it pays to buy the best quality feed available.

As a very approximate guide, a horse will eat up to 2.5 per cent of its total bodyweight each day. The difficulty arises when you try to divide this into bulk and concentrates. According to the recognised system, the bulk should be decreased in direct proportion to the increase in concentrates, and for a fit horse around 15.2 hh. this could result in proportions of up to 18 to 20lb of concentrates and only 10lb of hay – amounts that would have most endurance horses popping out of their skins.

Another way of putting it is to say that you would be feeding as much grain as you could persuade the horse to eat. In fact, riders can often be heard complaining that their horses will not eat enough concentrates. It is true that there are horses whose metabolisms burn up food at such a rate that they do need these high levels of concentrate feed. However, they are fortunately the minority, and anyone starting to train an endurance horse from scratch would be better advised to think of the feeding problem in a rather different way.

Feeding bulk as freely as possible keeps the horse occupied and prevents him from becoming bored; it also keeps his digestive system occupied, as nature intended, minimising the likelihood of digestive problems. Oats contain a high level of fibre compared to other grains and are therefore a safe source of energy on which to base a traditional diet. Use the best quality you can buy and preferably bruised or rolled. Bruised and rolled oats do not keep very well, so buy a maximum of three weeks' supply at a time. As you want the horse to be in good condition to start training, include in his diet fattening foods such as boiled or micronised barley and soaked sugar beet pulp, which will help keep his ribs covered.

The Manager's Eye

Always keep the level of exercise ahead of that of feeding, so you may start the horse on as little as 3 or 4lb of concentrate per day. By the time he is doing about two hours' work a day, in the early spring, this will have increased to around 6 to 8lb a day, depending on the size and type of horse. This is where the observant eye of the good horse manager comes in, relying upon the visual evidence of the horse's condition to tell him whether the diet is meeting the horse's needs. The things he looks at are the covering of flesh, state of skin, coat and mucous membranes, alertness of expression and condition of droppings, to name but a few.

Observe your horse's condition and adjust the quantities of each diet component accordingly. If he is getting too fat, cut down the barley; if he seems lazy, increase the oats and reduce the sugar beet pulp; if he is too full of himself and becoming unmanageable, go easy on the grain for a while.

Compound Feeds

If you really cannot obtain good quality traditional feeds, or if you cannot cope with mixing your horse's feed yourself, you can resort to one of the many compound feeds on the market. Some of these are specially formulated for high performance horses. They provide a balanced diet and usually include minerals and vitamins.

The snags with this type of feed are that while the food values are maintained, the actual ingredients may change from batch to batch, so you have less control over what your horse is actually eating. As they provide a balanced ration, they should not be mixed with other foods such as grain, as this would unbalance the rations. Some horses object to nuts for breakfast, lunch and tea!

Mixers and Additives

For a mixer, to stop your horse bolting his short feed, use either chaff or soaked sugar-beet pulp. Bran, the traditional mixer, has high levels of phosphorus and when combined with oats, which are low in calcium, it creates a calcium/phosphorus imbalance. Modern processing methods make it almost impossible to buy good quality broad bran these days, so it is better omitted from the diet. On rest days, however, the amount of concentrates should be reduced and a bran mash may be fed if desired.

The easiest way to increase the fat level in the home-mixed ration of your working endurance horse is by adding a couple of tablespoons of corn oil to his feed.

The addition of succulents, especially carrots, is a good idea if your horse cannot be turned out very often. A little molasses will tempt a really fussy feeder and may also encourage a horse to drink when he is away from home and the water supply is different.

General Points

When you are making changes to your horse's diet, introduce them gradually to give his digestive system time to acclimatise to the new food. Always dampen feeds to aid digestibility, reduce dust and avoid selectivity, and always give the horse time to digest his food before exercise.

When your horse approaches competition fitness, you may be feeding anything from around 8 to 15lb of concentrates per day, according to his individual needs and the level of competition. This amount may be less if he is turned out on good pasture every day. The important thing is to be observant. Learn to trust your eye to tell you whether your horse is getting the nourishment he requires, and don't worry because someone else's horse eats twice as much.

4 Care of the Feet

The best endurance horse in the world is useless if his feet are wrong, whether owing to a conformation defect, faulty action, injury, disease or bad shoeing. The stresses imposed on the horse's feet are enormous: think of the combined weight of the rider and the horse's own body, concentrated into the tiny area covered by the four feet, even when the horse is stationary. The pressure is considerably greater when the horse is moving.

The endurance horse, unlike the racehorse, does not move over a carefully prepared surface but over terrain which can vary from baked clay to deep mud, from soft sand to hard rock, and from grass to flinty shale. Often there are many variations within the course of one ride. He also competes, in general, without the artificial protection of support boots, bandages or pads, and must keep up the effort for anything from three to twenty-four hours, with the minimum of rest. It is a lot to ask!

Riders will go to great lengths to learn about every aspect of feeding and training their horses, but often know very little about how the feet work and move. Perhaps this is because horses' feet manage to cope despite all kinds of abuse, and the horses don't complain. Farriers may also be partly to blame; they often tend to assume that owners know nothing about their horses' feet, and don't encourage them to learn. Nevertheless, if you want your horse to perform, you must get to know his feet as well as you

know any other part of him, then persuade your farrier to give them the best attention possible.

The first thing to be aware of is that the horse's conformation affects the distribution of his weight through his limbs. Abnormal conformation may result in weight being thrown to one side or the other, or forwards or backwards, which in turn sets up abnormal stresses in the joints. This can exacerbate the situation, causing faulty action, injury, weakness in specific areas and eventually permanent damage. It is most important to realise that a problem in the foot will affect the rest of the body and vice versa.

The extent to which remedial farriery can improve the functioning of the feet depends upon the source of the problem. Problems resulting from neglect or bad shoeing can usually be resolved, while those resulting from an inherited defect, disease and sometimes from injuries, may have limited scope for improvement.

Therefore, when buying an endurance horse pay special attention to his feet, and if there is any room for doubt as to their strength and soundness, leave your money in your pocket and find another horse.

Good Endurance Feet

Each fore and hind foot must be a mirror image of its opposite. One larger than another, or a different shape, could mean that the horse has suffered some illness or injury which has left a residual weakness. Alternatively, the problem could be congenital and predispose the horse towards unsoundness later.

The feet must be well shaped, in accordance with the normally accepted good conformation of the foot. The forefeet will be rounder than the hind feet, with the hoof axis making a slightly more acute angle with the ground.

The horn of the hoof wall should be dense, hard and fine grained, without prominent growth rings. Where rings are apparent, they should relate to changes in diet or management of the horse. Beware of signs of laminitis. There should be no flaking or cracking of the hoof wall, which should be thick enough to give a good nailhold and bearing surface. The sole should be slightly concave, as flat feet are more easily bruised.

The frog should be well shaped with clearly defined central and side clefts. It should be large, healthy and resilient, all signs that it is doing its job of helping to expand the foot and reduce the effects of concussion. The bars should also be well defined. They give support at the heels and allow for expansion of the foot when it comes to the ground. The bars should not be cut away, as is sometimes done. This is a bad practice which leads to contraction of the heels and a reduced bearing surface.

Hoof and Pastern Slope

The slope of the hoof and pastern provides the equine equivalent of the suspension system in a car – the springs which prevent jarring and reduce concussion. Obviously, a short, upright pastern ab-

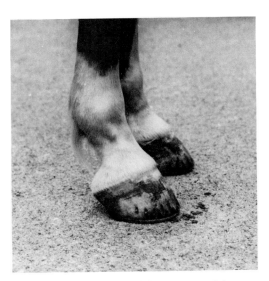

Fig 19   Good, well-shaped feet on an Arab horse, with the natural hoof/pastern axis more upright than on the Thoroughbred and with the pastern neither too short nor too long.

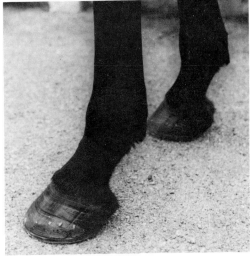

Fig 20   Good, strong feet on a Thoroughbred horse with a longer pastern, but the correct hoof/pastern axis maintained. The clearly visible rings denote variations in diet or management, probably according to the time of year.

sorbs concussion less effectively and gives a more bumpy ride than a long pastern which forms a more acute angle with the ground, has more room for movement and gives a more luxurious ride. However, the short pastern places less strain upon the tendons, while the long pastern places a great deal of strain on them. A balance therefore has to be found whereby the pasterns are sufficiently long to act as shock absorbers, but not so long that excessive strain is placed on the tendons. The generally accepted ideal is a hoof/pastern axis of 45 degrees in the front feet, slightly more in the hind feet. In their book *Endurance and Competitive Trail Riding*, Wentworth Tellington and Linda Tellington Jones found that in successful horses in the 1976 Tevis Cup Ride, the slope in the front feet varied from 48 degrees to 55 degrees, and in the hind feet up to 65 degrees.

It does seem that there is a tendency to prefer slightly more upright feet in endurance horses. This in turn means the shoulder will be more upright. Whether the benefit of alleviating strain on the horse's tendons outweighs the disadvantages of reduced shock absorption and restricted length of stride depends upon many other factors: type and breed of horse; length and scope of competition; type of terrain; the horse's fitness; and the rider's skill.

Bear in mind that a tendon injury is immediately apparent and may be remedied by rest, while the effects of concussion may take several years to develop and the damage may be permanent. The rider, in the meantime, continues, blissfully unaware that a problem is developing.

The line through the pastern and hoof which forms the hoof/pastern axis must be straight and parallel with the hoof wall at the front of the foot when viewed from the side. Any attempt to increase or decrease the slope artificially will result in breaking this line. However, where excessive growth has taken place at either

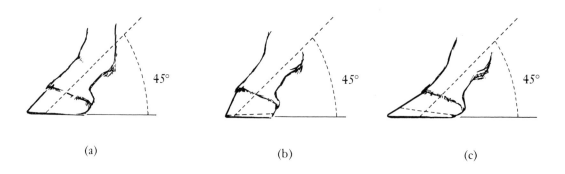

(a)   (b)   (c)

Fig 21   (a) *Normal hoof/pastern axis, based on the 'ideal' angle of 45 degrees. (b) Shortened toe, or overgrown heel, showing hoof/pastern axis broken forward. (c) Overgrown toe, showing hoof/pastern axis broken back.*

the toe or the heel, the axis will be seen to be broken either backwards or forwards, respectively, and the foot can be trimmed to restore the natural straight line.

From the front, the hoof/pastern axis should be a vertical line through the centre of the fetlock joint, the pastern and the hoof, ending at the toe. Any deviation from the vertical indicates either pigeon-toed or splay-footed conformation. A horse which is either pigeon-toed or splay-footed is likely to have other conformational defects in its limbs, which put added strain upon the joints.

Conformation

The conformation of the feet can vary from shallow and flat to upright and boxy. Shallow, flat feet are often found in Thoroughbreds. The horn is frequently soft or brittle and given to cracking or flaking. The pasterns are often long and acutely sloping and the natural long toe, low heel conformation is exacerbated by the toes being left over-long when the horse is shod.

Upright, boxy feet, by contrast, are more often found in Arabs and some cobs. The horn is usually dense and hard, the heels high and the soles domed. This type of foot can cause several problems: the bearing surface is limited and if the heels are shod too closely, as often happens, there is insufficient room for expansion of the foot. The frog does not come into contact with the ground and dies away through lack of use, shock absorption is reduced and other problems such as contracted heels ensue.

Action

The conformation of the foot is closely related to the conformation of the rest of the body, and both determine the horse's action in the various gaits. 'Normal' is the word used to describe the preferred combination of parts and the way they work to produce the most desirable result. This can vary according to the work required of the horse. In some breeds, for example, a showy, flamboyant action may be desired. The action of the endurance horse, however, is efficient, economical and capable of covering the ground – any ground – as quickly as possible. Any defects which prevent the horse from using its component mechanical parts to the utmost, with the minimum of stress and strain, are a serious disadvantage.

The endurance horse with 'normal' conformation will have straight, economical action. Each moving hoof will pass the stationary leg at the highest point of its arc of movement. The foot will come to ground heel first, with the toe straight. The forearm and knee will raise the foot sufficiently to clear obstacles on the ground, but not so high that time and energy are wasted. Normally, the hind feet will track up straight behind the forefeet, although some top endurance horses place their hind feet outside the track of their forefeet.

The shoes should show even wear. Uneven wear is indicative of a problem which needs investigation. Possible causes are conformation defects, abnormal gait (such as paddling, winging and plaiting), incorrect preparation of the hoof for shoeing or the wrong choice of shoes for the horse and the work. A registered farrier will know how to shoe a horse to minimise the effects of faulty

49

conformation or action. Notice how your horse's shoes wear and ask your farrier what can be done if there is anything you feel unhappy about.

Farriery

One of the reasons that foot and shoeing problems are often allowed to pass unnoticed by riders and owners is that their adverse effects on the health and potential working life of the horse do not become apparent in many cases for some time, perhaps even for several years. It is often only when a problem has been allowed to develop to the point where performance is acutely affected that any action is taken. In such cases the cumulative bone damage may be permanent, even if the correct

balance of the foot can be restored. Maintaining a correctly balanced foot, with a normal hoof/pastern axis and a level bearing surface is essential to the art of good farriery and to the sustained good performance of the horse.

Shoe Design

Most horseshoes used today are machine-made and the most frequently used design is the concave fullered shoe. The concave shape means that the shoe is narrower where it meets the ground than where it adjoins the hoof. This follows the natural shape of the foot, gives a good gripping edge and reduces the effects of suction in heavy going. The concave shoe is also lighter than a plain shoe.

Fullering, the cutting of a groove

Fig 22 Good feet and shoeing are essential to good performance. A well-balanced horse moving at speed on Exmoor.

around the ground surface, improves grip. The width of the shoe should conform to the natural bearing surface of the foot, and should cover the wall, white line and approximately ⅛ inch of the outer border of the sole. In general the shoe will be slightly wider at the toe, where the wear tends to be greater, than at the heels.

The thickness of the shoe depends upon the size required, but it should be uniform. The weight affects the horse's action, a heavier shoe encouraging him to pick his foot up higher and vice versa, and this can be taken into account when shoeing for training or competition. Some riders prefer to use a slightly heavier shoe for training on the basis that it also helps strengthen the horse's legs. Of course, a heavy shoe is also more tiring.

Corns

One of the most common foot problems found in endurance horses is corns. As the hoof grows the heels of the shoe move forwards off the wall and bars, pressing and bruising the space between which is known as the seat of the corn. Great care should be taken when the horse is shod to ensure that the heels are long enough and set back flush with the wall, and that they are not turned in too close (another common bad shoeing practice). Ideally the heels can be bevelled off at the same angle as the wall. If the horse is inclined to overreach, the front shoes can be pencilled, that is, bevelled off more obliquely. This minimises the chance of the shoe being caught and pulled off by the hind foot reaching forward.

Special Shoes

As a precaution against overreach, stumbling and forging, the farrier may suggest the use of shoes with rolled toes. Brushing can also be counteracted by the use of special shoes, which vary according to the area causing the damage. Brushing is the striking of the inside of a limb with the shoe of the opposite foot, and it occurs when a horse is tired, unfit or in some cases young and still immature. With correct training, as the horse reaches maturity or becomes fitter the problem will usually disappear.

There is an argument that to cope with the stresses and strains of endurance work a wider web shoe than usual is preferable. This could well be true in some areas, but on rough, stony ground, dry springy turf, or deep, holding going, there are obvious disadvantages. The grip on slippery going is less good, there is a chance of grit or gravel getting under the shoe and in deep going it is more difficult for the horse to pull his feet out of the mud so suction may loosen the shoe.

Studs and Pads

Where extra grip is needed, for example for jumping or riding on slippery roads, various types of stud can be used. However, the use of studs unbalances the foot, and although they may be helpful for the endurance horse at certain times, for example on frosty roads in winter, in general the disadvantages outweigh the advantages.

If studs are used, the plug type are to be preferred. These raise the heels less than other types and give improved grip on roads and rocky going. If you intend to use studs, use them throughout your training period so that the horse becomes accustomed to them.

Horseshoe borium (tungsten carbide crystals) is quite expensive, but when welded on will greatly increase the life of the shoes. Its possible disadvantage, which also applies to studs, is that by totally preventing slipping, the strain on the leg may actually be increased. Both schools of thought have supporters, and it is at present a matter of personal opinion whether anti-slipping devices are desirable or not.

Some long distance events permit the use of pads, while others do not. Although the success of some horses equipped with pads cannot be denied, it could be argued that if an endurance horse needs pads to protect his feet from bruising, he is probably not a very good prospect.

The problems of using pads are many. Firstly, in EHPS rides horses with pads are ineligible for gradings or trophies. Secondly, the presence of flexible material between the shoe and hoof makes lost shoes more likely; very careful packing of the space, either with tow or silicone, is essential to avoid grit or gravel finding a way in and causing trouble. Thirdly, there is an argument that the presence of the pad interferes with the natural concavity of the foot and decreases the horse's ability to grip on slippery, hard going, particularly if the frog is also covered.

Daily Care

Having ensured that your horse's feet are correctly balanced and well shod, it is important to give special attention to their daily care. Whilst you may be able to save time by cutting down on other grooming, never neglect your horse's feet.

Picking Out

To stay healthy, the feet need to be picked out twice a day – first thing in the morning and after exercise. It is especially important for stabled horses to have their feet picked out, as standing in droppings and wet bedding softens the horn and may lead to thrush – an unpleasant fungal infection that is invariably the result of bad management.

Hoof Dressings

Some people never use hoof dressings, others apply them religiously every day. The important thing to be aware of is that it is the correct moisture content which maintains healthy feet. Hoof oil or grease is impervious, and can either have the effect of preventing moisture from evaporating from the feet, or preventing too much moisture from softening the horn. If a horse is kept stabled, his feet dry out, and daily applications of hoof oil won't help unless the feet are first washed (or in extreme conditions soaked) to restore the moisture content. The dressing will then help prevent moisture loss. The hooves of horses turned out in fields in winter, on the other hand, may become softened through being continually soaked. It is then a good idea to apply a dressing before turning the horse out.

There are many proprietary dressings on the market and the best contain lanoline, a natural animal grease obtained from wool. Vaseline, however, will also serve the purpose. There is no evidence to suggest that the application of these dressings increases the rate of growth of the horn.

Cornucrescine is a specialist dressing sold specifically for the purpose of promoting the growth of horn. It acts as a mild blister and should be used only when specifically needed, and then not for longer than it takes to cure the problem. A more quickly grown horn may prove weaker and more susceptible to flaking and cracking than horn grown at the normal rate.

Considerable success has been achieved in improving the state of soft, crumbling hooves by feeding a supplement of biotin, one of the vitamin B group. Like all nutrients, however, it must not be considered a 'cure-all' in isolation.

Fortunately, there are a number of proprietary balanced supplements available through veterinary surgeons which may greatly improve poor feet. If your horse's feet are prone to cracking, splitting or flaking, you should consult your vet, who can advise on the best treatment.

Finally, remember: no foot, no endurance horse!

5 Health

The most successful endurance riders know their horses inside out. They spend enough time observing their horse to be aware of any small change in the horse's appearance, behaviour and attitude. They can take immediate action if something is not quite as it should be, whether that involves giving the horse a rest, adjusting his diet or calling the vet.

The Healthy Horse

A healthy horse has an alert, interested expression, with ears constantly moving to catch the sounds of his surroundings. His ribs will be well covered, even when fit, as his muscles will be hard and well developed. His skin will be loose and elastic, and his coat will lie flat, with an obvious sheen. His tendons will be cold, hard and free from any lumps or swellings, and he will move freely, with a spring in his step. His eyes will be bright, and the membranes lining his eyes, nostrils and mouth will be pink and moist. Normal droppings are firm, moist and smooth (neither too hard nor too soft), while the urine should be clear and pale in colour. A healthy horse will have an appetite to match.

Warning Signs

The horse owner should be aware of all these basic signs of good health and learn to be aware of any deviation from them. Warning signs may include a dull or staring coat, where the hairs are on end, due to the skin being stretched tight in illness; discoloured mucous membranes, abnormal droppings and urine, listless appearance, and poor appetite or refusal to eat. The horse may also drink considerably more, or considerably less, than usual. There may be a raised temperature; the horse's normal temperature is 99.5 to 101.5 degrees Fahrenheit. The pulse-rate may be elevated or abnormal, the normal resting pulse-rate being between 36 and 42 beats per minute. The respiration rate may be increased from the normal resting rate of between 12 to 20 complete breaths per minute.

To take a horse's temperature, a veterinary thermometer (available from your vet) should be shaken down until the reading is well below the 100 degrees Fahrenheit mark, then greased with Vaseline. Standing to the side of the horse, to minimise the chance of being kicked, raise the dock with one hand and insert the thermometer into the rectum. Rotate it gently and make sure that it touches the wall of the rectum. Hold it in place for one minute before reading it.

Pulse-rate can be taken with a stethoscope, just behind the elbow, or with the fingers, where an artery passes over a bone close to the surface of the body, such as under the jaw. A normal pulse has a rhythmic, two-part beat. The heart rate rises with exercise and stress, but should quickly return to normal once the cause of the stress is removed. Some horses have an abnormal heart beat with no

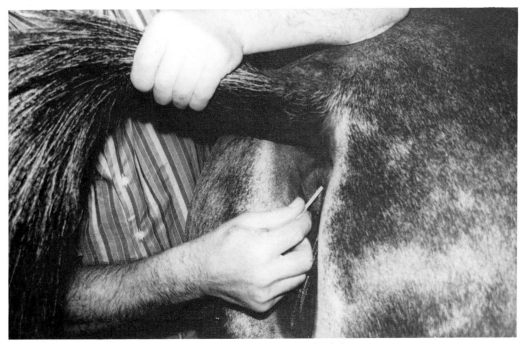

Fig 23   Taking the horse's temperature. Standing close to the side of the
horse minimises the chance of being kicked.

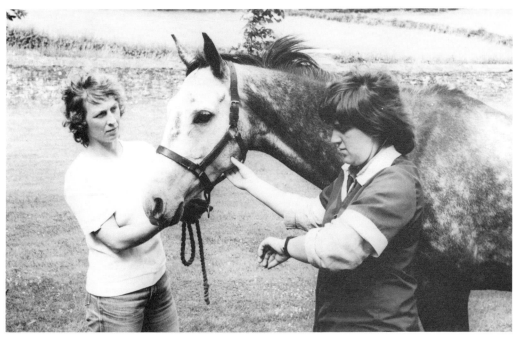

Fig 24   Taking the pulse by finding the artery under the jaw.

apparent ill effects; in others, an abnormality may be more serious. When a heart problem is suspected, expert advice should be sought.

Respiration rate can be checked easily by observing the rise and fall of the horse's flanks in normal conditions. However, a stressed or excited horse may pant, breathe irregularly, or seem not to breathe at all, making his respiration impossible to monitor. In the stabled horse increased respiration, or apparent difficulty with breathing, is a sign of trouble.

It pays to make a habit of observing your horse's general condition and behaviour until it becomes something you do automatically every time you enter his stable. A problem noticed in its early stages is usually more easily and quickly resolved than one left until it cannot be ignored.

Routine Health Care

Several aspects of your horse's health and well-being should be attended to routinely as part of good, general horse care.

Worms

Whether he is kept stabled or at grass, your horse should be dosed regularly against worms, particularly redworms, the most dangerous of these parasites. Where several horses are grazing the same pasture, regular worming is especially important; removing droppings from the pasture will also help to reduce the infestation.

It is impossible to eradicate the problem altogether, however, so all horses need a worming programme. It is re-commended that on average horses should be wormed every six to eight weeks, although the risk of worms is greatest during the summer, so more frequent dosage is required at that time than in the winter. In the late autumn, a wormer effective against the larvae of the bot fly should be used.

Teeth

If your horse develops a dislike of the bit or becomes fussy in his mouth, have his teeth checked. Once a horse has his full set of permanent teeth, from the age of five onwards, they should be examined twice a year by your veterinary surgeon and rasped, if necessary, to smooth away sharp edges.

'Wolf teeth', vestigial teeth which sometimes erupt just in front of the molars, can cause problems with bitting. Young horses often shed them along with their temporary teeth, but they can be removed surgically if necessary.

Innoculations

All horses should be innoculated against tetanus. The initial course of injections should be followed up with a booster at not more than three-yearly intervals. In case of injury, especially puncture wounds, a booster tetanus injection should always be given. Tetanus, otherwise known as 'lockjaw', is a distressing and painful disease from which very few horses recover.

Influenza vaccinations are now commonplace following their introduction as obligatory in racing (soon followed by other disciplines) to combat epidemics which disrupted sport. Influenza is highly infectious, and although new viruses which are resistant to the vaccine strains occasionally appear, anyone regularly travelling to competitions in other areas, should possess an up-to-date vaccination certificate. This is in any case a requirement at all major rides and at some others, especially where stabling is provided.

There have been reports of horses reacting adversely to influenza vaccinations, but these have not been proven and affect only a tiny minority of vaccinated horses. There is therefore no reason to avoid having your horse vaccinated. Each booster must be given within twelve months of the preceding vaccination. Choose a time for vaccinations when your horse is not competing or preparing for a ride, such as during his winter break. He should have a week's

rest from work following his influenza vaccination.

Equine Ailments

Some ailments likely to affect the endurance horse are digestive problems (including colic), azoturia, muscle and tendon injuries and strains, and bone and joint problems.

Colic

Colic, a term widely used to describe symptoms of abdominal pain, can occur in any horse and for a number of reasons. These include the consumption of unsuitable food, bolting food, irregular feeding, sudden changes in diet, too much

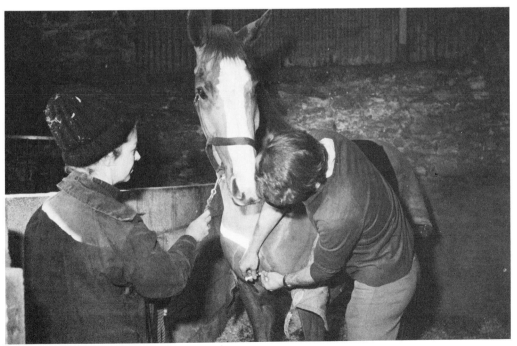

Fig 25   Keep vaccinations up to date.

cold water after exercise, exhaustion and dehydration, and a build-up of sand taken in by the horse when drinking from a sandy stream.

The most common cause of colic is the blockage of an artery by worm larvae, which results in damage to a small section of the gut and acute pain (spasmodic colic). When a blockage is involved the problem is known as impacted colic. In its severest form, a twist occurs in the small intestine and blocks it completely. In these cases surgery is essential, if the horse is to stand a chance of survival, but even then this condition is often fatal.

The stresses and strains of a long ride, dehydration and the interruption of a regular feeding routine caused by a competition, may all increase the likelihood of a horse getting colic. Organise your competition routine so as to minimise the risk, and stay alert after the ride. Do not put your horse away and forget about him until next morning, but check on him regularly until you are sure he is relaxed and settled.

Colic can usually be treated satisfactorily if it is spotted quickly. Symptoms are the outward indications that the horse is in pain - patchy sweating, pawing the ground, looking round and attempting to bite or kick the flanks, rolling, restlessness, shivering, lying stretched out on the ground and increased pulse and respiration. Don't take chances - call the vet.

Azoturia

Azoturia, or 'tying up', occurs when a horse on a high energy diet is laid off work without a corresponding reduction in his feed, then brought straight back into hard work. The glycogen stored in the horse's muscles is the initial source of energy. When there is a sudden, heavy demand for this energy, excessive lactic acid is produced which irritates the muscle fibres. The outward symptoms are: a shortened stride behind; stiffness, with eventual inability to move; muscle spasms in the hind quarters and loins, with the muscles becoming hard and painful; discolouration of the urine; sweating; increased pulse and respiration; and a raised temperature.

There may be other causes of azoturia and associated or similar problems, such as mineral deficiencies, a lack of vitamin E in the diet, and the horse's ability to metabolise certain foods more quickly than others. Research is currently being carried out to discover more about the problem. Meanwhile, the best chance of avoiding azoturia lies in good management of the horse's diet and exercise programme. Always keep exercise ahead of increases in food. Some horses are prone to azoturia and once they have had an attack, the problem is likely to recur. With quick diagnosis and the proper treatment a horse will usually recover, but he will need rest followed by a slow return to exercise and a carefully monitored diet.

Lameness

Lameness is the outward sign that there is a problem somewhere in one or more limbs, and it has many possible causes. Lameness is probably the most frequent reason for horses being eliminated from long distance rides.

Lameness may be due to an injury anywhere from the shoulder to the foot, involving muscles, tendons, ligaments or bones, but the most common seat of lameness is in the foot. Sudden lameness is usually due to an injury of some sort; this can be anything from a picked up nail or bruised sole, to a dislocation or a ruptured tendon. Intermittent lameness usually indicates other causes. It may decrease or increase with work and be accompanied by stiffness, hampered action and stumbling. Bone problems, ranging from splints to navicular disease, may cause lameness, as can ageing, arthritic joints. The most common causes of lameness in endurance horses are corns and stone bruises in the forelimbs, and pulled muscles in the hind limbs.

To treat any cause of lameness it is essential to make an accurate diagnosis. This is not as easy as it might sound, and expert advice is required. The serious endurance rider should learn as much as possible about how particular types of lameness indicate different problems, and should know how to tell which limb is affected. For example, with front-limb lameness, the head and withers of the trotting horse will rise as the lame leg meets the ground. With hind-limb lameness, the head is lowered and the point of the hip of the lame leg rises as it meets the ground. Riders frequently fail to notice lameness when two opposite limbs are affected, as the action of one limb matches the other. You should make a point of knowing your horse's normal, sound action.

Some horses have an odd or unusual gait which may seem unlevel, but which is not necessarily lameness. Experienced long distance vets often get to know these horses, but it is not unusual for their owners to be asked to trot them up twice at the pre-ride vetting. The moral of this is to buy an even-gaited horse, unless you want to lose weight, or get extra fit!.

6 Equipment for the Horse and Rider

Look at the competitors in any long distance ride and you will see bridles, saddles and riding wear of every description. One of the attractions of the sport is that you don't initially need a vast array of specialist equipment, but can use what you already have for general purpose riding. As you progress towards more serious competition, you will work out how specialist equipment can help you and your horse. For both of you, the primary consideration is comfort, since whatever tack and clothing you choose is going to be in use for anything from three to twenty-four hours at a time.

Saddle-fitting

The most important item of your horse's tack is the saddle. For any horse sport a well-fitting saddle is essential, and particularly so for distance work. A badly fitting saddle will not only cause galling, pressure bumps and a sore back, the discomfort of wearing it can easily spoil the horse's performance. The pressure of the saddle and rider on his back is quite enough for the horse to cope with, without the additional stress of a badly fitting saddle.

The best person to assess the fit of a saddle is a qualified saddler. The saddle should fit the contours of the horse's back, with a clear channel running from front to back and no pressure on the horse's spine. Too wide a tree will allow the saddle to bed down too far, with the arch pressing on the withers, while a tree that is too narrow will pinch the withers. The lining should be smooth with the stuffing even on both sides and free from lumps. A horse's shape changes during training and, as he becomes fitter, it may be necessary to have the stuffing adjusted to maintain a good fit.

Unsuitable Saddles

The endurance horse needs as much freedom of movement as possible, so keeping pressure off his back to allow him full use of his strong back muscles is a prime consideration. The rider can only do this if the saddle allows him to balance over the horse's centre of motion.

The saddle must be of such a design that it will place him neither too far back, nor too far forward. The forward-cut jumping saddle is designed for use with short stirrups and allows the rider's seat to slide backwards when jumping, while the old-fashioned English hunting saddle, with a flat seat, encourages the rider to sit too far back. Neither of these saddles are suitable for endurance work. It is also important to prevent excess weight being placed at the front of the saddle. This results in excessive pressure on the wither area, as happens with some deep-seated saddles used for dressage.

The 'Combination' Saddle

The ideal saddle will give the rider a deep, central position with a close contact, but will also allow the seat to leave the saddle comfortably. One type which seems to fit the bill is the 'combination' saddle, designed to be used for all three phases of event riding. This type of saddle has a deep, central seat, with a comparatively narrow waist and recessed bars. It allows a close contact but is forward cut, usually with knee rolls and a fairly wide seat so the stirrups can be shortened as required. During the course of a long distance ride you may wish to alter your stirrups, both to alleviate muscle strain and to take account of varying terrain – riding longer on easy going and shorter on rough, hilly ground. Stirrup leathers should be strong with sound stitching, and the irons of stainless steel as nickel is prone to stress and sudden breaks.

A spring tree saddle is probably more comfortable for the rider, but some competitors prefer a rigid tree, which is less likely to cause friction and pressure on the horse's back. Which of these you choose is a minor consideration, compared to the overall fit and design of the saddle.

Specialist Saddles

There are several specialist saddles on the market. Many riders use the Paragon, the first of these to be introduced, manufactured by John Goodwin International Limited. It is described as a combination of the British cavalry saddle and the

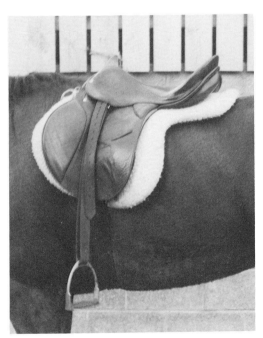

Fig 26   A good general purpose saddle.

Fig 27   The Paragon long distance saddle made by John Goodwin International.

American western saddle. The deeply padded seat makes this a very comfortable saddle for the rider, although the rider's contact with the horse is somewhat reduced.

The Endurance-LDR, by Equestrian Products Innovation Company Limited, was designed specifically for endurance riders. Its main feature is military-style, extended panels which maximise weight distribution. It has a high gullet, cut back head and deep seat. This affords a close contact, and requires a 'long leg' riding position.

Finally, the Glenn Hellman long distance saddle is a lightweight saddle based on a rigid tree. It has extended panels, a cut back head, and thick felt flaps and lining, externally covered in pigskin. There are no knee rolls and the seat design encourages a forward riding position, enabling the rider to get his weight out of the saddle. It also affords close contact with the horse. Valerie Long, twice winner of the 100-mile Summer Solstice ride, uses a Glenn Hellman saddle on her Arab stallion, Tarim.

Every style of saddle has advantages and disadvantages. In a top level class requiring a minimum weight of more than 11 stones to be carried, a lightweight saddle could be a disadvantage. On the other hand, a military-style, western or stock saddle might be too long for a short-backed Arabian horse, causing pressure on the loins. Provided the fit and seat position are right, it is up to the individual rider to decide what saddle best meets his needs.

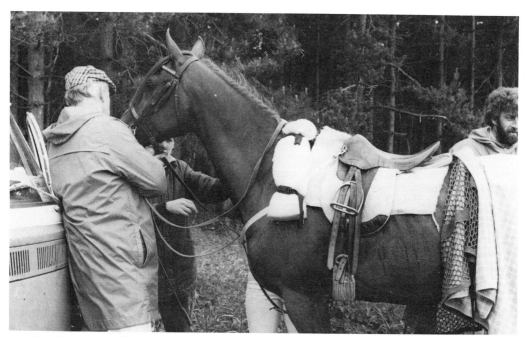

Fig 28   Val Long's stallion, Tarim, wearing an original Glenn Hellman saddle. In later models the felt flaps are covered with pigskin.

The Bridle

The choice of bridle is governed by two requirements: it should not rub, and it should be convenient. To prevent rubbing, the fewer straps involved the better, so on an ordinary snaffle bridle the noseband is often discarded. A traditional bridle of headpiece, browband, cheek straps and reins is perfectly adequate. However, it has to be completely removed and replaced with a headcollar at mandatory halts, so that the horse can eat and drink. This can cause problems if the horse is excitable. Some horses wear a headcollar under the bridle, but this again increases the amount of strapping and is not really the answer. Riding in a hackamore, or bitless bridle, does solve the problem, but not everyone wishes to do this.

A very practical bridle for long distance riding is the combination bridle and headcollar developed by EPIC (Equestrian Products Innovation Company Limited). It is made of rolled leather to reduce the possibility of chafing, and has a fixed noseband with a tethering ring so that when the bit is removed, the bridle acts as a headcollar.

Reins and Bit

Reins are a matter of personal preference. The webbing type with stops are practical and durable, do not slip when wet and are less bulky and more comfortable to cope with than rubber covered reins.

Bitting is a subject which could easily fill a book on its own, but there are a few key points to remember. Firstly, you will almost certainly want to change bits at least once during the course of a horse's training, depending upon his head carriage and muscle development; if he is over enthusiastic you may need extra 'brakes'.

Secondly, your endurance horse is essentially required to be a 'trail horse'. Most of the time he will need a free rein so that he can see where he is going, and can extend his head and neck as an aid to balance and breathing. The most the rider should do with the reins and bit is indicate direction and apply quick half halts. These will prevent the horse becoming inattentive, tripping over obstacles, or losing his balance and rhythm.

Thirdly the reins and bit should certainly not form a gadget to counteract pulling. Whatever the bit in the horse's mouth, any rein aids should be given quickly and precisely. If the horse does not respond, the aid should be repeated. Aids given incorrectly and maintained too long, encourage the horse to pull; he is simply reacting against the uncomfortable pressure of a meaningless drag on the sensitive areas of his mouth. The bit is not there to stop the horse running away, but to help define the rider's tactful requests.

Some riders begin a ride with a pelham or hackamore, then revert to a snaffle. Frankly, if a pelham or hackamore provides the little extra needed communication with a fresh horse, there is nothing to be gained by changing half-way through the ride. Once the horse has settled, the aids are needed less often – no bit is severe in itself, it is the way it is used that matters.

American endurance riders seem to prefer the mechanical hackamore to any kind of bit, while in England the German-style hackamore is gaining in popularity. The hackamore, or bitless bridle, has a strong action, so it is essential that it is fitted correctly. The noseband

Fig 29   Beltane Phoenix wearing a hackamore of the type favoured in Britain.

should be above the nostrils, the shanks clear of the chin and the chin strap about one and a half inches above the chin groove. It certainly has many advantages for endurance riding, but should not be used by inexperienced riders.

The action of the hackamore, pelham and various types of American western bits are all suitable for trained, well-balanced endurance horses, competently ridden. The snaffle, the favourite British bit, may work just as well for many horses, but it often needs to be used in conjunction with a drop noseband. A major problem with the snaffle is its mild action, which a fit and excited horse can ignore or lean on. Rein aids may need to be frequently repeated, with the possible consequence of a bruised mouth and penalty points, not to mention a tired rider.

Other Equipment

Girths

Many types of girth are suitable for endurance horses. Padded girths by Cottage Craft and Kangol have proved their practicality; Kangol's have a soft, absorbent cotton lining. String girths (not the nylon type) are favoured in America. Webbing and lampwick girths are going out of fashion as they are more inclined to rub, whilst leather girths need careful cleaning to keep them supple.

Whatever girth you choose, rubbing and chafing will be avoided by changing it regularly. The horse's girth area can also be hardened by daily applications of rubbing alcohol or surgical spirit after exercise. Girths should be rinsed well when washed, and care should be taken not to use a detergent which could irritate the horse's skin.

Numnahs

Numnahs must be changed and cleaned regularly, so you should have a minimum of three. The most practical kind are those made from soft polyester pile fabric, similar to that used in hospitals to avoid bedsores. These prevent jarring and rubbing, do not wrinkle and are machine washable. The best are generously cut and shaped to pull up into the gullet of the saddle. Sheepskin makes an ideal numnah, but only the most expensive, top quality products can be washed, so they are not really practical for everyday use.

The American 'cool back' pads are popular with some riders and are available from good stockists of western riding equipment. Many riders now prefer a woollen blanket, cut to size and folded double, or a woollen western-style saddle blanket, to a pre-shaped numnah. Wool, being a natural fibre, absorbs sweat and does not slip, reducing the risk of chafing. Cotton is also absorbent, but unless it is well padded it is inclined to wrinkle and cause pressure marks. Thin saddle-cloths and non-absorbent materials such as nylon are to be avoided.

Finally, remember that the purpose of a numnah is to provide overall cushioning whilst absorbing sweat, not to protect a horse from a badly fitting saddle.

Fig 30   A well-fitting saddle with the numnah pulled well up into the channel, avoiding pressure on the horse's spine.

Breastplates

The breastplate can be either an English hunting-style breastplate, or the American type, preferably the kind that is shaped to fit the chest. During training the horse's shape will change and it will be found that at some stages a breastplate is unnecessary, whilst at others, such as when training up and down steep hills, it becomes essential.

The Rider

Hats

As with the horse, the rider's competition wear should take into account the need to

Fig 31   Hard hats are not compulsory in the United States. This Tevis Cup veteran sports half chaps and a wide brimmed hat to give protection from the sun.

be as comfortable as possible for the duration of a long ride. The rules for both BHS LDR Group and EHPS rides in Britain now insist that hard hats are worn. Approved hard hats vary greatly in design, so it is worth shopping around for the most comfortable fit you can find.

Boots

Boots for endurance riding are a problem. Many American riders wear running shoes, but this is not advisable as the lack of a heel makes them unsafe for riding. Lightweight hiking boots and similar short boots such as desert boots are worn by some riders. Provided there is some protection for the rider's leg, they are practical both for riding and running alongside the horse. Chaps, thick, long socks, tights and leg warmers have all been tried, to protect the calf from chafing when short boots are worn.

On shorter rides, ordinary riding boots are adequate. However, the rubber ones are too hot in warm weather and too cold in cold weather, whilst the leather type are often not tough enough for the rigours of the sport – an important consideration when they have cost you a small fortune! Neither rubber nor leather riding boots are suitable for running. Jodhpur boots are better, but the soles do not afford much grip.

Other Clothing

Socks and other underclothing are best made from natural materials which absorb perspiration. Thermal wear which allows perspiration to 'wick' through to the outside is also suitable. Scratchy lace trimmings, seams at any point where the rider's body is in contact with the horse and anything which fits too tightly are all to be avoided.

Stretch jodphurs and breeches are more comfortable if they are cotton lined, though the British climate is seldom hot enough to make them uncomfortable. Riders in the 1985 Tevis Cup in California appeared in everything from jeans to vividly coloured tights and leotards!

A sweatshirt or similar loose, stretchy garment makes a comfortable top. Some kind of neckerchief is a practical addition, as it will keep out draughts, absorb perspiration and, in extreme cases, it can be turned round and tied over the nose and mouth to keep out dust.

Gloves are an essential item of kit. The rider's hands can become quite cold even in milder weather, especially early or late in the day, and gloves can make a great difference to comfort. Thin ones are best as they enable the rider to maintain a sensitive rein contact. The style is a matter of personal preference related to the type of reins being used.

Waterproof wear is also essential, whether it be a full length mac, or a jacket and over trousers. A mac keeps the saddle dry, but I personally find a long mac too bulky and prefer a waxed cotton jacket and trousers. Over trousers should have elastic stitched to the bottoms to keep them down over your boots. Waterproof materials range from PVC to GoreTex, but waxed cotton is still hard to beat for lightness and comfort during a long day.

Fig 32   Glenn Hellman on his Welsh pony Bucklesham Camilla wears a felt hat over his crash helmet, short boots and thick socks. Camilla is in a western bridle and a saddle designed by Glenn specifically for long distance work. She has a wool saddle blanket and there is a sponge tied to the saddle to wash her down.

7 Schooling and Training the Horse

If it were possible to lay down an exact formula for training a long distance horse, much of the fascination of the sport would be lost. It is the horse's individuality which really tests the rider's ability to achieve results. Of course, there is a limit to how much you can alter the basic material. What you should aim for is the best possible result with the raw ingredients available. To do this, you must know and understand what you are starting with, and what you can hope to achieve.

Although certain breeds and types of horse are preferred, long distance riding of some standard is within the scope of virtually any kind of horse. Many horses have been unexpectedly successful, most notably Margaret Montgomerie's Irish cob Tarquin, veteran of thousands of competitive miles and still going strong at 23. He certainly does not appear the ideal horse one would choose for distance work. However, he has a marvellously economical ground covering action and an owner whose knowledge and skill have made the most of him. The endurance horse is principally a trail horse and he and his rider must learn to work in harmony and look after each other. For the horse this means balance, alertness, responsiveness and obedience.

Schooling

Many horses used in distance work are less successful than they should be for two reasons: lack of correct basic schooling and the rider's inability to maintain balance.

Balance

The single most important factor is that the horse is well balanced. No matter how fit he is, if he is unbalanced physical problems related to undue stress will eventually catch up with him.

When a horse is running free, it is easy to see that his forelegs and shoulders bear most of his weight. His head and neck are stretched forward to help balance that weight, while the main function of the hind legs and quarters is to propel him forwards. When the horse is first ridden he finds the weight of the rider awkward. We refer to the young horse new to carrying a rider as 'going on his forehand'. This means that he has not yet strengthened his back and adjusted his body to carry the unnatural additional weight of the rider.

This adjustment cannot be made all at once. Like the human, the horse needs

Note   Source of information on fitness training in this chapter is The Veterinary Clinics of North America, Equine Practice, Vol. 1, No. 3 (December 1985).

considerable time to alter and strengthen his muscles, ligaments and joints to take on new work comfortably. This is the purpose of basic schooling – to alter and strengthen the horse's physique so that he can carry a rider with the minimum stress and the maximum comfort. Correct basic schooling takes into account the horse's physical structure and how it can best be developed to carry a rider.

If a horse does not receive the correct schooling, he will invent his own techniques of making the presence of the rider less uncomfortable. He will attempt to evade the rider's weight as far as possible, without learning to support it comfortably. The result of this is invariably an 'upside-down' horse, with a hollow back, heavy muscle development under the neck and an inclination to snatch the reins from the rider because he is unbalanced. His back muscles will be undeveloped and he will be unable to bring his hocks

underneath himself to create impulsion. A correctly developed horse pushes himself along from behind, whereas an unschooled horse pulls himself along from the front.

Approach to Schooling

It is much easier to train a young horse from scratch than it is to retrain an older horse who has been allowed to develop incorrectly. However, with perseverance and careful work a degree of improvement can be achieved.

The first thing to assess is whether your horse is capable of carrying his rider in a balanced way. If not, you will need to assess what you know about his previous training and current stage of development before deciding what to do. A young, immature horse needs progressive work, without too much being asked at one time. If you are starting with a

Fig 33 Balanced horse with rounded outline and natural self-carriage.

Fig 34 Unbalanced horse with hollow outline, raised head carriage and build-up of muscle on underside of neck.

three- or four-year old, you can expect to spend three or four years bringing him on before attempting serious endurance work.

If you have an older horse and want to introduce him to distance work, he can work much harder, but he must be worked correctly: concentrate all the time on controlled, free forward movement, straightness, rhythm and relaxation, resulting in improved balance and better co-ordination. This is achieved by working to improve the horse's strength and suppleness.

With a young horse, schooling begins with working on a circle, on the lunge without a rider. Initially, this is designed to get him used to the idea of working, to help him relax and to begin the process of making him supple and strong. Ridden schooling involves the performance of

Fig 35 Kay Trigg's Brookhouse Maestro moving freely on Exmoor.

various exercises in a controlled situation, working towards a specific end result.

There is not room here to discuss basic schooling in detail, but there are many good books available on the subject. The basic schooling of a horse is not a job for a novice rider, and if you acquire your first horse as a youngster, you will be saved much time and trouble later if you invest in some experienced help at the start of his career.

The basic points to remember when schooling your horse are that he should be straight, balanced, forward going, relaxed, attentive and moving with even, rhythmic steps. These are essential requirements whatever his stage of training and without them no further progress can be made. In the endurance horse, we are not looking for the degree of collection needed for dressage. However, a mature, balanced horse should be able to work in a reasonably collected outline when asked. There is a tendency for distance riders to concentrate so much on forward movement at speed that their horses become overbalanced on the forehand and don't have the chance to develop their back muscles sufficiently. Such horses often have difficulty coping with steep hills.

The endurance horse needs to be able to turn in balance, to change direction quickly in response to weight and leg aids, to move forwards or sideways off the leg when asked and to make rhythmic, balanced transitions both upwards and downwards. Endurance riding is tiring for both horse and rider. A well-schooled horse, who is obedient to the aids, wastes none of his own energy and makes life much easier for his rider. A horse who fights you for the first fifteen miles of every ride is wasting energy.

Fig 36 School work is never wasted.

Ridden Schooling

The controlled situation of an enclosed school or paddock is an essential part of training. It helps focus the horse's attention on his work and enables the rider to concentrate solely on the horse and his way of going. However, a great deal of schooling can be achieved out on rides, if the rider pays attention to the horse rather than the scenery.

Frequent transitions from walk to trot and back to walk can be practised virtually anywhere; concentrate on making them as smooth and precise as possible. Use half halts, give and take with your hands as necessary and use your legs and seat to maintain rhythm and impulsion. If you want to stop for any reason, your horse should not shuffle to a stop but make a good, square halt, remaining attentive and on the bit until you tell him

he can relax. You can practise lengthened and shortened strides, leg yielding and other movements that will be useful in competition, such as opening and closing gates correctly and quickly.

Explore your local territory and find every useful hill, pathway or piece of common land that could help add interest to your riding. In particular, make the most of hills. Hill work strengthens muscles and improves balance as well as increasing stamina. Steep hills and rough terrain will replace a great deal of the formal work that would otherwise be necessary in the school to improve suppleness and balance. Don't be afraid to push your horse through rough terrain. He will have to cope with it in competition and it will teach him to concentrate and be attentive. Of course, you will need to take care on hard or stony ground.

Fig 37 Going uphill – Pat Amies on a relaxed Rufus, in a good riding position, with heels down and weight forward.

Fig 38 On the way down – Pat Amies with heels well down and weight slightly inclined forward.

Fitness

For many years horses have been 'made fit' for hunting, racing and eventing following traditional methods because they have been found to work, without much understanding of why they work or exactly what effects they have on the horse's body. Success or failure is put down to the mysterious innate skill of the horsemaster, or lack of it. In fact, the horsemaster's skill is no more a mystery than any other acquired ability. The great horsemasters were successful because they cared enough to study their charges. They took the time to stand and look over the stable door, to observe small changes in condition and attitude, to consider what might have caused them and to act accordingly.

Basic fitness training has remained much the same, but now we have the benefit of a great deal of recent research into exercise physiology which helps us understand what we are trying to achieve. Progress is being made quickly in this field and over the next few years we can expect more exciting developments.

Components of Fitness

Fitness is the horse's ability to produce absolute peak performance on the day of a competition. What this 'fitness' involves varies according to the discipline, so that fitness for the endurance horse will not be the same as that for the dressage horse. The potential to reach a certain state of fitness becomes obvious during training, so whilst two horses may start training towards endurance rides, one of them may turn out to be more suited to competitive trail riding, or another sport altogether, because of his physiological make-up. One important result of recent research has been to explain how the physiology of the horse with endurance potential differs from that of the horse better suited to sprinting.

Fitness may be separated into three component parts – suppleness, strength and stamina. Suppleness goes hand in hand with co-ordination and balance. Schooling exercises stretch and bend the various parts of the body to improve the elasticity and resilience of muscles, ligaments and tendons, producing greater co-ordination, a more refined response, and reducing the risk of injury.

Strength involves the development of muscular power and a corresponding increase in the resistance to stress of all supporting structures – ligaments, tendons and bones. In assessing a horse's potential strength, bone density and conformation are the important considerations. Extra size does not mean extra strength; a bigger horse takes much longer to mature and may well be more prone to joint and tendon problems than a smaller horse. Acquired strength depends upon managing energy production and utilisation effectively.

Stamina is the most important aspect of fitness for the endurance horse. It involves the production of energy to fuel the muscles which provide the locomotive power and keep the horse moving at speed for long periods of time. Stamina depends upon the efficient working of the respiratory system, which takes up oxygen, and the cardio-vascular system, which transports it to the muscles, where it is used to convert food nutrients into energy.

Fitness Training

The purpose of fitness training is to adapt the horse's bodily systems so that they can produce more energy without the horse becoming stressed or fatigued to the point of distress. However, the application of stress in controlled amounts induces the changes in the horse's body which enable it to increase its energy production and perform better.

Training involves: provision of sufficient food nutrients for the work re-required; good stable management to maintain the horse's general bodily health; progressive amounts of work to increase the horse's capacity for energy production; and specific types of work designed to increase stamina, speed and endurance.

All the horse's bodily systems are involved in producing the end result which is a horse who can successfully complete a ride at a specified level (and in top level endurance rides, achieve a placing) and be passed by the vet as 'fit to be ridden'. The digestive system converts food into a form in which it can be stored by the body until needed, either as fatty acids or glycogen. The respiratory system provides the oxygen necessary for the chemical conversion of nutrients into energy, and the cardio-vascular system circulates the blood which carries the oxygen and nutrients to the muscles, where this conversion takes place. The energy thus created enables the muscles to stretch and contract, exerting a force, via the tendons and other connective tissue, which manipulates the joints and results in the mechanical movement of the limbs. The whole process is controlled and co-ordinated by the brain, acting through the nervous system.

Energy Production

Energy is produced both aerobically (using oxygen) and anaerobically (without oxygen). No form of exercise relies entirely on one means or the other. However, anaerobic energy is mainly produced when short bursts of energy are required. This might be at the onset of exercise before the aerobic metabolism has gone into full production, for short distance sprinting, or when the oxygen supply is insufficient to fulfil the horse's needs aerobically.

The anaerobic metabolism utilises glycogen in the muscles as its fuel. It produces lactate as a by-product, and it is when the glycogen stores become depleted and lactate production becomes excessive that fatigue sets in.

The aerobic metabolism takes longer to come into play than the anaerobic metabolism, but it is a more efficient means of producing energy for extended periods of time. Therefore it is the aerobic capacity for energy production which is important for the endurance horse.

Research indicates that all horses have an in-built ability to produce the short, sharp bursts of energy which are mainly anaerobically produced. The potential for aerobic energy production can be improved by increasing the horse's ability to use oxygen, which is the main purpose of training.

Two types of fuel are used to produce energy aerobically – fatty acids and glucose, with fatty acids being the preferred source. This is why endurance horses are thought to benefit from a high fat diet, once they are in full work and training.

Muscle Physiology

Muscles are made up of bundles of fibres controlled by motor nerves. There are two main types of fibres – slow twitch and fast twitch, so called because of the time it takes them to reach peak tension. Fast twitch (FT) fibres can be further sub-divided into FTa and FTb fibres.

Slow twitch (ST) fibres are mainly involved with prolonged, low intensity work, such as endurance work, while FTb fibres produce short, sharp bursts of energy as required for sprinting. FTa fibres come into use as endurance work progresses, followed by FTb fibres. In racing, however, almost all the fibre types are employed from the outset.

ST and FTa fibres are able to utilise oxygen efficiently while FTb fibres are more suited to anaerobic energy production. Research indicates that the muscle fibre types are probably determined genetically and do not change as a result of training. It has been found, logically, that top endurance horses have a higher proportion of ST and FTa fibres, while racehorses tend to have a higher proportion of FTa and FTb fibres.

It follows that the more ST and FTa fibres there are present, the greater inborn potential a horse will have for endurance work. However, peak performance depends upon the increased and sustained ability of the bodily systems to utilise oxygen for energy production. Exactly how this ability may be limited is not yet understood, but it has been established that increasing the duration, intensity and frequency of exercise in training does increase the body's capacity for aerobic energy production and prolonged low intensity work, whilst delaying the onset of fatigue.

Devising a Training Programme

First Steps

The aim of training is to increase the horse's capacity for aerobic energy production and thereby his capacity for endurance work. How can this be achieved?

When starting with a horse from scratch, the first essential is to ensure that he is basically healthy and able to cope with the demands of a training programme. When brought in from grass he should be wormed, his teeth should be checked, his feet attended to and he should be examined for any unsoundness. A blood test can be done if there is anything which gives cause for concern.

Secondly, you must realise that in order to undergo specific performance training, a horse needs to have a solid base of general fitness. Before trying to get a horse fit for a 50-mile (80 km) endurance ride he needs to be 'hardened off' enough to cope with the increased demands of the work.

Training should therefore begin slowly, as for any other discipline. It should start with walking which, although usually called roadwork, need not all be done on the roads if you have somewhere nicer to ride. A certain amount of work on hard surfaces will, however, help to strengthen the horse's legs. This phase should not be hurried. Too much trotting too soon on hard roads may cause concussion problems and, frequently, splints. Some gentle trotting and basic schooling can be introduced towards the end of the second week.

If a horse is very soft, half an hour's work is enough to begin with, working up to an hour after two weeks, then slowly increasing the time. After six weeks the horse should be capable of working steadily for a couple of hours each day. Lunging may be very useful at this stage, to relax the horse and encourage him to stretch his neck and back muscles as well as making him more supple.

A horse who has previously been very fit and has simply been let down for a break will come back into hard work much more quickly. Experience will tell the individual owner how much work his horse needs.

Progressive Training

Once the horse is hardened off and ready to go on to performance training, you can begin a programme designed to get him fit for a specific goal. At this stage it is important to realise that training for endurance rides must be progressive. In other words, the overall time taken to train a horse for a ride of 100 miles is proportionately greater than the time taken to train him for 50 miles. A seasoned endurance horse may come in after his winter break and be ready to do a 40-mile Golden Horseshoe qualifier in two months, whereas the novice horse will need six weeks hardening off, then two months' specific training for the same qualfier. As a very rough guide, add another month for 50-mile rides other than endurance rides and a further month for 50-mile endurance rides. Rides between 50 and 75 miles require a minimum of four months' specific training and 100-mile rides a minimum of six months.

Training involves the application of controlled amounts of stress in order to force the horse's bodily systems to at-tempt more than they would normally do. The repetition of this process is what gradually increases the horse's capacity to cope with and recover from the work. The factors involved are: time – how long each unit of exercise takes and the period over which the exercise is repeated; distance – increasing distances of training rides to build up to competitions and then going on to longer competitions; frequency – how often the horse is exercised; intensity – the level at which the work is carried out, including speed particularly, but also intensive schooling, or other activities such as jumping.

The time required extends into years, as top endurance horses improve season by season; it is commonly believed that it takes three years for a good endurance horse to reach his peak performance level. This is where the skill of the rider comes in – there are no hard and fast rules in training and no short cuts. The rider must assess the amount of work needed without doing too little or too much. He must keep the horse sound and healthy, devise a training programme and be able to stick to it or adjust it as required, and the effort must be maintained over a long period. Progress must be monitored and it is a good idea to keep a record of everything pertaining to the horse – exercise taken, innoculations, farrier's visits and especially any problems or injuries. It is most important that the owner develops powers of observation and an awareness of his horse's condition, attitude and changing performance levels.

Built into any training programme should be an extra time allowance in case the horse needs to be laid off work for any reason.

Performance Training

Performance training must include steady work, building up to the level required in the competition at which you are aiming, plus fast work to improve the functioning of the heart and lungs. Always warm your horse up at the start of a strenuous training session.

When a horse is working, his heart rate increases, the rate of increase depending upon the intensity of the work. When he stops working his heart returns to normal, between 36 and 42 beats per minute. It has been established that a horse's heart rate needs to increase to over 200 beats per minute to improve the functioning of the cardio-vascular system.

The speed at which the heart rate returns to normal is commonly used as a guide to the horse's fitness level. It is one of the parameters used in the veterinary judging at rides and can be used by the owner during training to assess the horse's progress. As he becomes fitter, his heart rate should return to normal more quickly. In some cases the normal heart rate may also decrease slightly. The heart rate should return to normal within half an hour after peak performance has been demanded, whatever the stage of training reached.

Immediately after a training ride, the heart rate will usually be found to have fallen to around 60 beats per minute and it should then reduce steadily over the next ten minutes or so. If the heart rate remains persistently high after work, it is an indication that the horse has been over-stressed, or possibly that something else is wrong.

Your horse's training programme should still include a variety of work when specific performance training be-gins. Schooling in particular should be maintained to keep the horse balanced and supple. Variety will also keep the horse interested and alert. He will quick-ly become sour and disillusioned if all that ever happens is another long training ride, especially if your space to ride is limited.

Ride Training

You should aim at having your horse fit enough to complete easily his first com-petition ride without stress. This means that before the ride you will want to know that he can achieve both the dis-tance and the speed comfortably. Most horses in a reasonably fit condition, but not specifically trained for endurance work, can cope with rides of 20 miles with no ill effects. Beyond that, the demands of long distance work begin to exceed the demands normally placed on the riding horse, so it is at this point that specific performance training really be-gins. Work out suitable training rides of varying known distances, combinations of say, 5, 8, 10, 15 and 20 miles. These can be worked out quite easily from a large scale (1:25,000) Ordnance Survey map.

Plan your training schedule on the basis that before a competitive ride of 30 miles, such as a CTR or a Bronze Buckle final, your horse will be coping easily with 10- and 15-mile rides by two weeks before the competition, at speeds slightly higher than those required for the event. Two weeks before the competition, aim to do at least one longer ride of about 25 to 30 miles at approximately the required speed, and one week before the compe-tition do another long ride, for example 20 to 25 miles at about one m.p.h. faster

Fig 39 Pauline Holloway coming in at the finish of a 40-mile qualifier on Clementine.

than the required speed. Exactly what you do and when you do it will be determined by the progress your horse is making and what you feel he needs in order to be ready for a competition.

Basic Principles

The basic principles to remember are: build up to longer, faster rides gradually; there are no short cuts – don't skimp on training time, as if your horse is to be fit enough to compete he must have done the necessary work regularly during the training period; don't ask too much during the week immediately preceeding a ride. It is too late then to catch up on lost work and the horse needs the time to 'charge his batteries' ready for the competition.

Once you are into the swing of things with a 30-mile ride under your belt, apply the same training principles to longer rides, remembering to take into account the competition work the horse has done when planning future training schedules. Competing will, of course, also improve his fitness.

Choosing your Competition

At some point you will have to decide what type of ride will be your main aim. This does not mean you can only do one type of ride, but the decision will influence which aspects of training you concentrate on most. For example, you may decide that CTRs are your forte, in which case, as you progress, judgement of speed will become a more important factor in your training. At present the maximum distance for EHPS CTRs is 60 miles, with set speeds up to 9 m.p.h. If, on the other hand, you decide that endurance rides are your main interest, distance will become the first priority, with speed taking second place until you and your horse have gained enough experience and fitness to want to go for a placing.

The fitter your horse becomes, the easier it is to keep him that way. Once he is competing regularly and achieving distances of 50 miles with ease, he can be ridden less frequently at home, perhaps five days a week instead of six, and he can occasionally have a rest of several days. During very early training, when you are competing in rides of 20 to 30 miles, your horse should be covering a total of around 40 miles a week. To build up to a 50-mile ride you should increase this to about 70 miles a week, consisting of one long, steady ride, one long, fast ride and three shorter rides.

By the time you start thinking about one-day 75 or 100-mile endurance rides, your horse will probably be competing in two- or three-day longer distance rides and training will take account of this. At this stage, with a number of longer distance competitions now on the calendar, anyone competing regularly can build up a horse's ability to cope with the longer distances as much in competition as in training rides at home. This also has the benefit of keeping the horse interested.

The atmosphere of a competition is much more conducive to useful work than trying to slog out 60 miles on your own. Again, there is no fixed rule as to how much work a horse needs before he can tackle a one-day 100 miler. By the time you reach this stage you should be able to assess the matter for yourself, based on your horse's past performance. If you find yourself contemplating such a ride with no idea whether your horse is fit enough to make a good attempt of it, then forget it and tackle something else until you are more sure of his capability. On

the other hand, remember that in endurance rides there are mandatory halts, with veterinary checks for the benefit of the horse's welfare, so you can always pull out, even if it is disappointing to have to do so.

Assessing Speed and Pace

Speed

Two things you will have to learn are how to judge speed and how to pace your horse. Judging speed is easily learned by experimenting with your training rides. Work out the distances between various points on the ride, maybe at five-mile intervals, and then work out how long it should take you to reach each point, given a required speed for the whole ride. If possible do this over varying terrain.

You will find that when you attempt the ride, some sections will take you longer and some less time than anticipated. During the course of a ride, you will proceed sometimes considerably faster and sometimes considerably slower than the required speed. It therefore pays, when you set out to do an important competitive ride, to know as much about the course as possible, and to find out where time is likely to be lost and where it can be made up. Roads and rough going with steep hills, or holding going, will slow you down quite considerably and any fast or easy going must be used to full advantage.

Get to know your horse's optimum speed at the various gaits – walk, trot and canter. This is the speed he easily travels at when fit, without having to be pushed unduly. Work out a set distance, preferably one mile, over fairly easy going and see how long it takes your horse to complete it at the different gaits. Repeat the exercise several times, not necessarily on the same day, to find the average.

Pace

Pacing the horse is another matter; it takes experience and is unfortunately a problem with the novice endurance horse, as horses also learn to pace themselves. This is why it is so important to teach your horse to maintain a good rhythm. Once a rhythm is established, he is less likely to burn himself out too early in the course of a ride. We will take a look at these aspects when we consider how to ride a competition.

8 Fitness for the Rider

Books on horse training frequently ignore the subject of the rider's fitness, assuming that a rider will see to it that he is fit enough for whatever he proposes to do. Rider fitness is more important for some disciplines than others; the fitness requirements for jockeys and event riders differ considerably from those for dressage and showjumping. Nevertheless, all types of riding require a basic level of fitness to make them enjoyable, and the fitter a rider is, the better equipped he is for success in his chosen sphere. In addition to basic fitness, the rider must think about 'riding' fitness. At its simplest, this means riding often enough to avoid suffering aches and pains as a result of your ride.

Until recently, endurance riding standards did not seem to warrant much concentration on rider fitness. However, with standards at the top steadily rising, the fitness of the rider has become a more important aspect of the sport. Increasingly, riders at all levels are making greater efforts to get themselves fit, either working out to a regular routine, or taking their exercise in a more haphazard fashion. There is, at least, a growing awareness that the rider must be fit enough to help, and not hinder, the horse.

Fitness Factors

The first consideration is that the rider should maintain a basic level of health and fitness. The factors involved are diet, rest and relaxation, and a maintenance level of exercise.

Diet

There is a tremendous awareness these days of the importance of a balanced diet, and it is not difficult to work out a straightforward eating regime that is easy to manage. In general, wholefoods are good for you, while too many refined or processed foods are not. Aim at fibre from fruit and vegetables to fill you up, rather than 'stodge' from biscuits and puddings.

Try to have regular meals, including breakfast, and don't make your last meal in the evening too heavy. Eat sensible but controlled amounts and work to achieve your optimum weight, then maintain it. There are many charts which tell you what your weight should be for your height and build, but the way you actually feel and your energy level will give you as good a guide. Don't binge every day, but eating an occasional Mars bar or slice of treacle tart is no crime! Some lucky people can eat 'like horses' without putting on weight; the rest of us have to be more careful.

Don't forget that your weight will also affect your horse's performance and the way you ride. Training together will eventually show you the optimum weight at which you can comfortably compete.

Rest and Relaxation

Rest and relaxation are also important to basic health and fitness, as it is during sleep that the body carries out its routine maintenance and repairs. Relaxation has more to do with mental well-being, in that it is a chance to relieve the tensions of the day's work and refresh your mental energies by doing something different. If you want to approach relaxation seriously, you could try yoga or meditation. Gardening, fishing, or hundreds of other activities might work just as well – the point is to take your mind off day to day worries.

Exercise

Exercise, in this context, means something other than riding, something that uses different muscles and works all the bodily systems to keep them functioning well. It could simply be walking, or it could involve one or more other sports. Swimming is excellent, or you could try cycling, tennis, badminton, squash – anything that gets the circulation going and improves your general sense of well-being. It is often a good idea to join other people for this type of exercise; part of the benefit is in the fun of doing it, so if you can make it a social occasion, so much the better.

Riding Fitness

The serious endurance rider, like the horse, needs suppleness, strength and stamina.

Suppleness

Suppleness is important because stiff joints and slack muscles which have lost their elasticity are most susceptible to injury when placed under strain.

Regular bending and stretching exercises will improve suppleness and should present no problems for someone with a good basic level of fitness. These exercises should be done smoothly and rhythmically (just as we want our horse to work in rhythm,) without any sudden or jerky movements. Such exercises are useful for warming up before going on to more strenuous things, as they start the body working without strain. They include, for example, toe touching, shoulder shrugs, side bends, leg swings and calf stretches. The latter are particularly useful for endurance riders: stand at arm's length away from a wall with feet together and hands together on the wall. Keeping your feet flat on the floor, lean forward, bending your arms, then straighten up. Relax and repeat. This exercise and many others suitable for riders can be found in *Fit for Riding* by Richard Meade (*see* bibliography).

Improved suppleness also leads to better co-ordination. For the rider this means reacting and applying the aids more precisely and consequently better communication with the horse.

Strength

Strength is the development of muscular power and is needed to maintain your riding position for long periods, thereby being better able to help your horse throughout a long competition.

Strength can be improved in two ways, either by body-building exercises which

Fig 40   Suppleness, strength and stamina are needed in the rider as
much as in the horse.

are best done under supervision, or, more practically for most riders, by exercises which also improve stamina, such as swimming, skipping and jogging. The important thing to remember with this type of exercise is that it must be done regularly, rhythmically and repeatedly to be of benefit.

Stamina

Stamina is the ability to work continuously without fatigue, and is therefore the most important factor for the endurance rider. It relates to the efficient use of oxygen and improved functioning of the heart and lungs. Aerobics, the recent fitness craze, are simply stamina building exercises, although they also develop suppleness and strength. Swimming, running, jogging, cycling and skipping are all good stamina build-ing exercises. The object is to increase the

pulse-rate, in much the same way as the horse's pulse-rate is increased during work, and to expand the lungs. It has been found that training has the effect of reducing the resting pulse-rate in human athletes.

Always warm up slowly when starting to exercise – it prepares the body for what is coming and reduces the risk of injury. Exercise regularly, beginning gradually and increasing the amount progressively. Never continue if something starts to hurt, although the point of most exercise is to continue until you just begin to feel the strain, then relax. If you are suffering from any illness or medical or physical problem, ask your doctor's advice before commencing any exercise programme.

For the endurance rider, sustained ef-fort is most important. A tired rider loses concentration, his reactions slow down, his muscles stiffen up and he becomes unbalanced; he needs to grip with his knees in order to stay in the saddle. This in itself is more tiring and also unbalances the horse. Harmony, rhythm and co-ordination are lost and coping with an unbalanced, tired rider puts stress on the horse at the very time when he most needs his reserves of energy. The horse is in more danger of stumbling, he takes less care of himself and the rider is in more danger of a fall.

In case of falls, it is a wise precaution for riders to have some first-aid training – you never know when an accident might happen miles from the nearest check-point. If you must fall, it is worth knowing how to do it properly to avoid jarring and minimise the risk of injury, although it is not suggested that you practise by actually falling off your horse! There are other ways of learning, such as lessons in judo or other sports where falling is involved. The important thing is to stay as relaxed as you can and roll when you hit the ground.

Riding Skill

Fitness for riding includes the rider's ability to communicate properly with the horse, that is, his riding skill and know-ledge. Long distance riding has frequently been left behind other disciplines in this area; the original idea was that the horse did the work and the rider didn't need to be particularly skilled to enjoy the sport. However, with standards rising, the rider's ability to help the horse

Fig 41   Sustained effort – a lone rider on a long hill in the Black Mountains.

may easily make the difference between the successful completion of a ride, and elimination.

We have already established that the horse must be balanced, rhythmic, straight, forward going, attentive and obedient, but it is the rider's job to achieve these things. The rider, like the horse, needs balance first and foremost. This means the rider's position and movements must cause the least possible disturbance to the horse, and his weight must be placed over the centre of motion to minimise interference with the horse's own balance. A good rider continually makes tiny adjustments to his position, imperceptible to anyone else, to remain in perfect balance with the horse.

With a balanced position, the rider can use his weight, legs and hands, in that order, to give precise and meaningful aids to the horse. Without balance the aids will be uncertain, often jerky and confusing to the horse, and he will react accordingly.

A balanced rider can help his horse travel through rough terrain and encourage him when he is tired, with the minimum risk of injury and the maximum chance of being passed as fit by the vet at the end of the ride. An unbalanced rider is an uncomfortable burden, making the horse's job more difficult. This is not the place for a lesson on how to ride, but if you feel that your riding could be better and you aim to compete seriously, begin by taking some lessons. Top riders in all the main disciplines recognise the importance of having a trainer on the ground.

9 Horse and Rider Relationship

Many riders, and some riding teachers, become so involved with what they are trying to do when riding that they totally ignore the much more enlightening aspects of *how* they do it, and why it does or does not work. In particular, they are inclined to ignore what the horse thinks about being ridden and this is a pity because the horse is one half of the partnership which they are working to improve.

Good Relationships

Let us first take a look at exactly what we mean by a 'good relationship' between horse and rider. Essentially, we want the horse to do all that we ask of him, willingly and without question, behaving in what seems to us a sensible and intelligent fashion. We accept that our part of the bargain is to ride as well as we can, in the happy belief that this will make

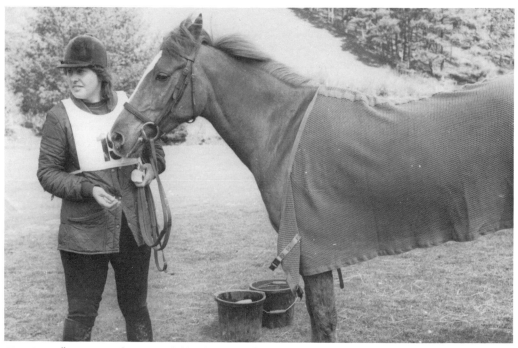

Fig 42   Sally Scorey and Squire Tebeldi relaxing briefly at the half-way halt on the Golden Horseshoe.

the horse perform better, though often we are reluctant to admit that our riding is not as good as it could be.

Regardless of how good or bad our riding is, if the horse objects to anything we ask of him, we blame him, and the more strongly he objects, the more we blame him. Eventually, if the matter is not sorted out, we begin to refer to the horse as a 'problem horse', because of the manner in which he shows his objections, such as biting, kicking or running away.

The endurance rider has an advantage when coping with horse problems. The fact that you will necessarily spend a considerable amount of time in your horse's company gives you the opportunity to study him and get to know him extremely well. All that time should not be wasted.

Understanding Your Horse

We often try to treat our horses as if they were human beings and expect them to behave as though they understand the world from a human point of view. This is a mistake. Horses may be highly intelligent – some are certainly more intelligent than others – but they can only use their intelligence in a way that makes sense to a horse.

Horses do not have the human power of reason. Their reasoning is based on a simpler way of looking at things, and they are far closer to nature than human beings. Historically, the horse developed as a range roaming creature of the plains. His main concern was survival: finding food, water and shelter, avoiding predators, mating and rearing the next generation. Wild horses today still roam in this way and have the same basic concerns.

The domesticated horse, although he has learned to tolerate and even, at times, to welcome the presence of man, is little different from his wild brethren. He does not have to search far and wide for food, water and shelter and his natural inclination to roam is curtailed by stable walls and field hedges, but if you watch a horse grazing in a field you will see that he is constantly on the move. In the wild he may have been at risk from lions or wolves, but he does not differentiate between one danger and another. To the horse, wild or domesticated, everything unknown is dangerous and since he is not well equipped to stand and fight, his immediate reaction to danger is to flee from it.

Communication

Everything in a young horse's life is potentially dangerous until he learns otherwise. His rider will expect him to do many things and accept much that nature never intended: he will be ridden, transported around the country in a noisy contraption on wheels and asked to carry on working beyond his natural inclination, as on a long ride. Therefore it is up to us to show him, in a way that he is able to understand, that it is all quite safe and can actually be a pleasurable experience.

Learning the Horse's Language

To reassure the horse, we must be able to communicate with him. This means that we, with our powers of reason and understanding, must learn his language, for he cannot learn ours. Horses have their own, very explicit language, as you will see if you watch a group of horses

87

Fig 43 Horse talk – a youngster submissively greets his ridden friend.

going unhindered about their daily business. They have ways of showing pleasure or annoyance, of amusing themselves and learning through play and of administering their own social hierarchy.

Lucy Rees, in *The Horse's Mind*, goes into great detail on how horses communicate and how to interpret their behaviour, facial expressions and vocal sounds. She also explains how 'pecking orders' are established and this is of great importance to the rider, who must act as the leader in the relationship in the same way as an older horse may exert his dominance over a youngster, or a stallion over his mares.

By learning the horse's language, which we can do during the hours we spend in his company, we can communicate with him in such a way as to build up his trust in us, dispel his natural fears of anything new, teach him to accept our lead and thus to respond willingly to our wishes.

The fact that the horse does not think like a human being does not mean that he is stupid. He merely works things out from a completely different starting point and this is what we must bear in mind all the time in our dealings with horses.

Problem Horses

Those horses condemned as problem horses are usually the more intelligent type of horse. Anyone who is involved in training horses will tell you that the more intelligent a horse is, the more difficult he is to train. Hot-blooded horses, the type we need for distance work, tend to be the most intelligent of all and therefore need

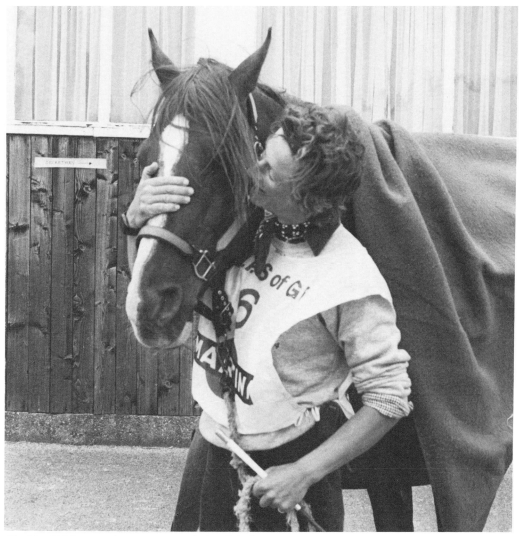

Fig 44   Val Long with Tarim. Correctly handled, the most sensitive horse can become calm, sensible and happy.

the most careful handling. Arabs in particular often have an undeserved reputation for being unmanageable, yet the horse of the Bedouin was so docile that he lived as part of the family. Problems, then, are usually in the mind of the rider, not in the mind of the horse.

If you watch competitors at a ride, it very soon becomes evident that a calm, happy rider and crew invariably have a calm, happy horse, whether or not the horse is of the hot-blooded, intelligent type, or the heavier, less highly-strung sort. Conversely, a tense, nervous and irritable rider, constantly on edge and nagging at the crew, will make the horse tense, nervous and irritable too, not to mention giving the long-suffering crew cause for complaint!

Inexperienced Riders

The lesson from all this is to cultivate calmness and relaxation. Remember, many problems are the result of inexperienced riders, keen to compete and do well, buying horses they cannot manage. If you are nervous of your horse in any way and do not feel relaxed and confident while riding him and attending to his daily needs, you need help.

Horses are large, strong creatures and they may often do things in reaction to their natural instincts which unnecessarily alarm inexperienced owners. On the whole, they prefer not to cause trouble or harm their handlers, but if the handler behaves in a nervous manner, this communicates itself to the horse. The horse, who is sensitive to danger, then thinks there is something to worry about. It does not occur to him that you are worried about what he might do to you! His reaction is to become tensely alert, looking for the danger. This means he cannot concentrate on what you want him to do and your efforts to gain his attention irritate him. If, on the other hand, you had approached him calmly, he wouldn't have suspected any danger and you could both have carried on as normal.

Competition Nerves

By the time you are into serious competition, fear of your horse should not be making you tense. But perhaps your problems start when you get to a ride; the tension of competing turns you into a nervous wreck and your normally equable horse into an unmanageable nuisance.

Cultivate calmness and consciously try to relax. Breath deeply and keep your voice calm. In other words, let your horse know that there is nothing to worry about; this is meant to be fun. Smile – it relaxes the facial muscles.

Controlling Your Horse

When ridden, the horse reacts to the tiniest tension in the rider, often without the rider realising it, and the usual reaction is for the horse to go faster, resisting the bit and the aids. A tense rider lacks coordination and balance and is uncomfortable for the horse, in addition to arousing the horse's ever present alertness to possible danger. His natural reaction is, of course, to run, and if there are other horses also running all around him, why shouldn't he believe there is something to run from?

In an endurance ride you want to be in control, not helplessly following where the other competitors lead. To achieve this, you need to develop your relationship with the horse to the point where he will listen to what you tell him. This is only possible when there is no tension barring your means of communication. When training your horse you should be constantly working on this developing relationship.

In the school, don't just think about your own actions telling the horse what to do. Try to feel all the horse's actions and be aware of the interaction between you. Consciously relax in the saddle and notice how your horse slows down. An excellent book on how to improve your riding is Sally Swift's *Centred Riding*. It is ideal for the distance rider as it aims specifically at developing the rider's inner awareness, extending it to his horse and their surroundings, and thus to the whole relationship between the two.

When you are out on a training ride, notice how your horse reacts to his surroundings, learn to anticipate his reactions and so absorb them without losing balance, concentration or rhythm. Practise using your weight to change direction, using your legs to keep the horse balanced, so that you can ride on a free rein. Allow the horse full use of his head and neck, particularly when moving at speed.

Listening to Your Horse

Learn to listen to your horse. Most horses enjoy competing and quickly learn what it is all about. Riders are frequently surprised that their horses learn to look for route markers and often spot them before the riders do. Listening to your horse could prevent you getting lost! There are some disadvantages, however. My own horse, and I am sure there are many like her, firmly refuses to

Fig 45   A tight turn on the 1986 Summer Solstice Ride, but note that
Val Long, wearing No. 7, has Tarim on a completely free rein.

believe there is any need to work hard when there are no markers in evidence, which makes solitary training at speed rather difficult. Horses learn many things as they become accustomed to competing. One rider told me her horse only has three activities – eating, sleeping and competing.

Energy conservation becomes an important factor in the top endurance horse's life. A horse who is going to improve in the sport soon learns to pace himself. If you listen, he will let you know when he wants to slow down or quicken up and you can learn to allow him to work within his natural rhythm and paces, whilst also working to improve them.

Many riders are afraid to give their horses a free rein in case they stumble, especially on rough ground or steep hills, but horses are very good at taking care of themselves and soon learn to co-operate with a sensitive rider in picking the best ground and keeping out of trouble.

Never underestimate your horse's intelligence and he will often amuse you as well as surprise you. On a long ride my horse discovered that a group of parked cars *en route* meant a checkpoint, water and other goodies. By the end of the ride, she was slowing down as she approached them and actively looking for our crew, evidencing much disgust on the two occasions they were not scheduled to appear!

10 Planning for Competitions

Preliminary Arrangements

At the start of the competitive season, or earlier, you will be thinking about your competition schedule for the year ahead. This is the time to make sure that your subscriptions are paid, your horse registered (for British Horse Society rides) and to check on anything of an administrative nature that might need sorting out before your first ride, such as horse vaccination certificates or trophy registrations.

Making Your Entries

The British Horse Society Long Distance Riding Group will send you a supply of ride entry forms once your horse has been registered. It also publishes a complete schedule of the season's rides. To enter a ride, you simply complete an official entry form and send it with a stamped addressed envelope to the organiser.

The Endurance Horse and Pony Society also publishes a fixture list and you send stamped addressed envelopes to the organisers of rides that interest you, for a schedule and entry form. Always return a large stamped addressed envelope with your entry for any ride, whether EHPS or BHS LDR Group. This is so that the organiser can send you all the ride details, such as a route map, route description, your number, vetting time and start time. The envelope should be at least large enough to take a sheet of

A4 paper folded double.

Some rides are better organised than others, but they are all organised by volunteers who put in a lot of time and effort and without whom the sport would not be able to continue. The least a competitor can do is read the schedule carefully and comply with its instructions.

When you send your entry off, make sure you have included all the information required on the form and always print names of riders and horses in block capitals. Be very clear about your own and your horse's eligibility to enter a ride when this information is required and if you have any queries about qualifications or other matters, telephone the organiser.

Choosing Your Rides

Choosing which rides to enter will involve a number of factors. Firstly, the age of your horse and your own degree of experience will dictate the level of ride you should be aiming at. An experienced rider with a trained horse might be planning a series of qualifiers and endurance rides, while the newcomer will be looking at Bronze Buckle standard and shorter distance novice Competitive Trail Rides. Young horses are usually introduced to the sport through a series of CTRs and training rides. The actual type of ride you enter will depend on whether you belong to the BHS LDR Group, or to the EHPS, or to both as many riders do.

How many competitions you enter and how often, will depend upon your travelling facilities, the location of rides and your other personal commitments, such as work or family needs. The number of rides on the calendar is increasing every year, but a horse needs a break between rides. For shorter distance rides this is not so important as they can be looked upon as training rides and most horses should be able to cope with them relatively easily. Once you are competing in fast CTRs and endurance rides of 50 miles upwards, you will need to leave at least three weeks between major competitions to give the horse an opportunity to recover from one ride and recharge his batteries for the next.

Some horses recover from the stresses of competition more quickly than others and seem little affected by fatigue. However, if you are lucky enough to have this type of horse, it is even more important to watch out for problems and to avoid overtaxing him. If a horse has had a hard ride, particularly early in the season, or if the going has been unusually tough, extra time between rides will be needed to make sure he is fully recovered. There are now enough endurance rides on the calendar to ensure that if your plans to enter one are thwarted, you can always enter the next on the list. Shorter distance rides take place most weekends during the season.

Ride Logistics

The next important thing to plan, once you have received your ride information, is the practical side of the operation. For BHS LDR Group rides over 30 miles, the rules require each rider to have a helper who is 'capable of taking charge of

Fig 46   Watering places often make good meeting points for rider and crew.

the horse' (juniors riding with an adult can share a helper). Helpers are not mandatory on EHPS rides, but they are advisable on rides over 30 miles where veterinary checks take place during the ride.

The job of the helper, or back-up crew, is to be available in as many places as possible throughout the ride, equipped to tend to the needs of the horse and rider, deal with emergencies and provide general help and encouragement. At mandatory halts a good crew will be able to take over your horse completely and attend to it exactly as you would yourself. Meanwhile, you can take the opportunity to relax and have something to eat and drink.

What you want your crew to do and how you want them to do it should be worked out before the ride, so that on the day there will be no hiccups. There are, however, certain variables. The way the horse is handled will depend upon conditions on the ride – he will need different care on a hot day than on a cold, windy day. Things may also happen on the ride which only you know about: the horse may feel lame for a while, or stumble, or seem to be tiring so that his pulse-rate rises. Such matters will have to be reported to the crew so they will know what to look for when checking the horse over. A good crew is invaluable and on really long rides it helps if you can have a couple of people who will muck in and help, keep each other company, encourage you and follow your instructions.

Fig 47 Don Haney relaxing in the shade at a halt on the Tevis Cup Ride, whilst his crew look after the horse.

Fig 48   A mandatory halt – the crews take over the horses and all the necessary equipment is carried in the back-up vehicle.

Equipment

As well as the equipment needed by you and your horse on the ride, your crew will have to carry a great deal more which will be needed *en route*. For shorter distance rides, when you may not have a crew, you will still need much the same equipment to look after your horse at the start and finish of the ride.

It is a good idea to work out a master check-list of all the equipment that you will need for rides. Keep it handy, then each time you load up all you have to do is go through the list. This is a much less nerve-racking way of doing things than getting half-way there and wondering if you packed the spare numnahs or the electrolytes. You will add your own ideas to the list, but basically it should look something like the following.

Rider's requirements
Crash hat and silk
Riding boots (and short boots in case it gets hot)
Jodhpurs (at least two pairs for any ride over 50 miles, especially for rides over two or three days)
Two or three changes of top – sweaters, sweatshirts and T-shirts
Suitable underclothing with complete changes as necessary
Cotton and woollen socks
Neckerchief and supply of large clean handkerchiefs
Gloves
Wet weather wear
Whip (if required)
Safety-pins, string, elasticated bandage for emergencies
Map, map carrier, compass, hoofpick, pocket-knife, money for telephone, sponge for washing down horse on ride

Horse's requirements

Bridle and bits (spare bridle if possible in case of breakages)
Saddle
Saddle cloths and numnahs
Girths
Stirrup irons, leathers and spare set of leathers
Breastplate
Other tack if needed, for example martingales, crupper
Rainsheet, blankets, cooler
Travelling gear: leg protectors or bandages, hock and knee boots, overreach boots, gamgee or leg pads, tail bandage and tail guard, anti-sweat sheet, travelling rug, roller, poll guard, headcollar and leadrope, haynet, water for journey if needed

Additional gear to be carried by crew

Water carriers and water
Buckets for drinking, washing down and feed
Feed
Electrolytes, salt
Stethoscope for checking pulse at halts
Spare set of horseshoes, the right size, obtained from farrier
Hammer and rasp
Food and drink for rider, including a thermos of hot drink, plus plenty of cold drinks according to preference
Grooming kit: dandy brush, body brush, sponges, sweat scraper, hoof pick
Towels for cooling out horse
First-aid kit: horse and human
Fly repellent
Equiboot (some riders carry them attached to the saddle)
Torch
Strong cord for running repairs, knife
Map of area

Additional requirements for overnight stays

Mucking out tools
Extra feed for horse
Tack cleaning kit
Night rugs
Bedding if not provided

At the Event

Arriving at the Competition

Allow yourself plenty of time when travelling to a ride – it is better to arrive two hours early than two hours late because of a breakdown or other delay. Arriving early also gives you and the horse a chance to unwind from the journey and relax before the ride. You can get things organised, collect your number, find out if there are any changes to the route or other matters you should know about, greet friends and generally make sure everything is properly prepared.

Don't take chances when travelling your horse. Protect his knees, hocks, legs and heels, use a tail guard and, particularly if you use a trailer, a poll guard. Most endurance horses quickly get used to travelling, but if you have a reluctant loader at first, it is worth spending some time on teaching him to load more willingly. Your horse may enjoy competing, but it can be most frustrating if he doesn't want to go home afterwards.

When you arrive at a ride, follow the instructions you have been given. If an overnight stay is involved, particularly at a racecourse, you will be required to show your horse's vaccination certificate before being allowed to unload. It is worth repeating how important it is to have these papers complete and up to date. Many horses have been turned away from rides because their papers were incomplete and the correct procedures for vaccination against equine influenza had not been carried out.

Find out which stable has been allotted to your horse, unload him and settle him down. Straw is usually provided, or shavings by prior request on your booking form, but if you require any other form of bedding you will probably have to take your own. All other equipment and feed (including hay) should be taken with you from home.

If the ride does not involve an overnight stay, as is usually the case, unload your horse and tie him up safely to your box or trailer, with a haynet within reach. Most horses are anxious to be out once they arrive at a destination. Leave your helper to see to the horse while you collect your number and any other information about the ride. You will usually be required to leave a small sum of money or your membership card as deposit against the safe return of your number. If you are riding without a helper, collect your number before unloading – do not leave your horse unattended outside the box.

Vetting

Be ready for your preliminary vetting. EHPS rides require the horse to be presented in a headcollar, while for the BHS LDR Group rides a bridle is required. The horse should not be tacked up, but you can keep his rugs on until the vet is ready for him, then quickly remove them.

Fig 49   A portable corral in use at Squaw Valley, before the Tevis Cup Ride.

Once vetted, you can return your horse to his stable if the ride starts the following day. If it is a one-day competition, tack him up ready for the tack inspection and the start of the ride. Rules regarding permissible tack vary considerably between the two organisations, so read them carefully.

Pre-start Check

Once mounted, check that you have everything that you might need with you. You might have been given a previously arranged start time, or you might be allowed to start when you are ready. For endurance rides, there might be a massed start, although if you wish to start alone this will usually be permitted. Check your watch – the starter will give

you your start time – so that you can keep track of how the time is going on the ride. You should already have worked out how long you aim to take to reach each checkpoint.

The Briefing

For major rides there is usually a competitors' briefing after the preliminary vetting, the evening before the ride. Both you and your helper should be there to avoid any communication problems which could completely upset your plans. If both of you attend, you can double check the information together and avoid mistakes.

The briefing will usually include a 'talkround' of the route, with an opportunity to ask questions and clarify any

Fig 50   Alison Kent gives the briefing during the 120-mile BHS Ridgeway Ride, July 1986.

uncertain points, plus details of any changes or external factors, such as road diversions or compulsory walking sections. You may also encounter a diverse range of interesting obstacles on the ride, so it is as well to know about them in advance!

The briefing may also include matters such as safety procedure if you get lost in open country and any local by-laws or landowners' requirements that you need to know about. Missing the briefing could spoil your chances of a successful ride, not to mention the trouble it causes for other people. Be there.

Other Arrangements

Arriving the day before a major ride gives you some opportunity to go out and have a look at the route, get an idea of the going and sort out the best places for your crew to meet you. Crews have the chance to orientate themselves and check the shortest road routes for meeting their riders. If the information is not provided, always ask how often water is available on the route, so you have an idea of how much you need to carry with you.

Make sure your crew knows what your planned ride tactics are – roughly what speed you are aiming for, where you aim to make up time and where you plan to ease up. In this way, your crew will have a better chance of being in the right place at the right time and will be able to keep a check on your progress.

When you depart after the ride, thank the organiser and leave the stable in the condition in which you would like to find it.

Fig 51   Christine Hull, one of Britain's top riders in recent years, with her horse William, and husband, David, who crews for her.

11 Completing the Distance

Priorities

Whatever ride you are competing in, your first priority should be to finish with your horse 'fit to be ridden'. If you complete the distance and pass the veterinary test at the end of it in any endurance or long distance ride, you will have achieved what you set out to do. A win or a placing in an endurance ride is a bonus, while in a standard or competitive trail ride it is better to be content with a completion or a low grading, than to be eliminated. If you do win a medal, or the Grade 1 you are aiming for, so much the better.

Knowing Your Limitations

You should know your horse well enough to recognise when he is about to become over-stressed and be prepared to slow down accordingly. You may have prepared him as well as you know how, but on the day something may not be quite right – perhaps you couldn't give him quite as much work in the previous weeks as you know he should have had; perhaps he is simply feeling off colour, as horses sometimes do; perhaps you are feeling off colour and just aren't riding as well as you usually do. Whatever the reason, accept the situation, work to a lower goal, or be prepared to withdraw if your horse is giving cause for concern. Off-colour one day may be indicative of impending illness. Once you have worked out what went wrong, you can concentrate on improving it and things will be better next time. Meanwhile, because you have not tried to push your horse beyond his limits, he will still be sound and ready to be worked on, even if there is one less trophy on your sideboard or rosette on your wall.

This is the essence of distance riding. At any major ride you will find experienced competitors who have withdrawn for no appreciable reason that you can see. The reason is nearly always the same: 'I could feel he was tired' or 'It just wasn't going well, and I wanted a horse left for tomorrow'.

Endurance Rides

There are riders (and horses) who have been on the endurance scene year after year and there are others who appear suddenly and do incredibly well for a season, or even a couple of rides, and are then never heard of again. A good horse can give an inexperienced rider a taste for the rewards of the sport – excitement, success, that well-known adrenalin high – then, because the rider has not known how to put in the basic groundwork, things go wrong. The willing, quality horse who lacks further training will work himself too hard and become seriously lame, or will perhaps become exhausted on a ride and tie up, or get a bad attack of colic. The rider then becomes disillusioned and gives up endurance riding.

It is the fear of this kind of problem that

deters many people from attempting endurance rides at all, whilst they will enter every CTR they can find. This is a pity, because once a rider has gained enough experience to do well regularly in shorter distance rides, he is well equipped to go further and apply his knowledge to training for an endurance ride.

Horses in endurance rides in Britain undoubtedly receive better care during competitions than those in any other sport. The rides provide a tremendous opportunity to really get to know your horse, plus the challenge each time you ride of testing your ability against your previous best.

There are, of course, placings to be had in endurance rides, but when winning trophies becomes more important than the challenge of a tough ride, it is time to give up endurance riding. To the committed endurance rider, a completion rosette from a tough ride will always be of more value than an easily won gold medal.

Planning for Success

Whether you are setting out on the Golden Horseshoe Final or a 20-mile CTR, success will depend as much on how well you plan your ride and how well you stick to your plan as on the

Fig 52 Happy riders Jan Lloyd Rogers and Valerie Hayward on the way to completing the Red Dragon Ride.

weather, going and terrain.

Some endurance rides have massed starts but most start in groups of up to half a dozen riders, while in a few riders start singly. Newcomers to the sport need never worry that they will have to cope alone. There is always someone willing to share your company and you will meet many other riders on the route, as most short distance rides have large entries. The shorter distance rides are usually well marked, either with flags or with fluorescent tape and lime.

Knowing the Route

It used to be considered that course marking was less important than map reading; the onus was on the rider to find his way, and course markers were merely a guide. However, with rising standards and faster times continually being sought and achieved, it has been recognised that good course marking is vital.

Although the rider should, for his own benefit, familiarise himself with the route beforehand, maps are nowadays seen as an insurance against getting lost. There is no time to consult a map continually, but if someone has moved all the markers, as sometimes happens, your map and your prior exploration of the route will be invaluable in keeping you on the right track. Memorise as much of the route as you can – you will then notice more quickly if you go wrong.

You can investigate the route in three ways: by working it out from a large-scale map before the ride; by memorising any route description that may be provided; or by exploring the actual ground. If you can combine all three, so much the better. It is well worth investing in the appropriate large-scale Ordnance Survey

map as the route map supplied by the organiser is almost certain to be a small-scale photocopy, good enough for identification of the route, but not for picking out details of topography and landmarks. If a route description is not provided, work out your own, carry it with you on the ride and memorise as much as possible.

Take particular notice of hills, which will be shown by contour lines on large-scale maps, rough terrain and roadwork, all of which will slow you down. Also work out where you can make up time on good going.

Riding in Company

A novice horse benefits from steady company on a ride and it is a good idea to arrange to ride with someone with a similarly paced horse. Riding with a companion will help a novice horse to settle into a rhythm and may prevent him becoming upset when other competitors pass him, and vice versa. Forget about perfect gradings and optimum speeds on your first rides. Concentrate on riding with balance and getting that all-important rhythm going.

At this novice level, if you have a horse that has any potential in the sport, you are more likely to be covering the ground too fast than too slow, except on rides where the terrain or going is really tough. On CTRs even experienced riders find themselves waiting outside the finish until sufficient time has elapsed to bring their overall speed down to within the accepted limit. If you have gone very fast and your horse is not tired, you will have made the pleasant discovery that most horses find 20 miles a comfortable ride, even if the rider needs to be fitter.

Fig 53 Lesley Dunn heads for home on her Arab stallion Bonanza.

If, on the other hand, your horse is very tired, and is perhaps eliminated with a high pulse-rate, take a good hard look at him. This should not happen and there must be a reason for it. The usual reason is that the horse is overweight and soft – something which is rectified by training – but if you thought the horse was fit when you started out, there might be something more serious amiss. A horse in normal work should be able to cope with a ride at this level with no trouble at all, and most do.

Developing Ride Technique

By the time you have completed a few rides you will be getting used to the way your horse copes with competitions and working out ways to make the most of his good points while minimising the problems. You will know, for instance, if he is likely to be over-excited and difficult at the start, wasting energy. You will know what his recovery rates are like and will be learning how to organise your riding to pass the veterinary test with the least likelihood of trouble.

At this stage you will be experimenting. Does your horse go better in company or does he settle better alone? Is he a natural leader or does he prefer to be given a lead? Remember that some riders can be justifiably irritated by another horse pounding away at their heels throughout a ride. If you are to benefit from another rider setting a pace, it is only fair that you should occasionally take your turn in front to give the other horse a break and some moral encouragement when he is tired.

If your horse starts a ride at speed when he is fresh, does it sap his energy later? Or does it make little difference? Is your training programme giving you the results you want? If not, why not? When should you progress to bigger things?

The answer to the final question is that you should move on when your horse has proved to you that he is ready and able to do so. When he is coping regularly with 40-mile rides, within his capabilities and without any signs of stress, you can think about venturing into endurance riding proper.

Ride Tactics

Two kinds of tactics come into play in endurance riding. The first are the tactics of riding for a completion, keeping your horse sound and unstressed. The second are the tactics of outriding the opposition, if you are aiming for a placing. This does not necessarily mean riding faster than the opposition – riders who do that often burn their horses out before the end of the ride – but riding a better planned race than the opposition.

Riding for a Completion

Completing a ride is the first priority and there are several ways in which you can give yourself and your horse a better chance of doing just that.

In rides where you start in small groups or singly, an excitable horse will probably pose less of a problem than in massed start rides. If you really don't feel confident about starting your horse in company, in most rides you can ask to start alone. Make the request on your

entry form. It is better, however, to get your horse used to company, as otherwise you are likely to have trouble every time you meet someone else on the way. Your horse will usually realise after a few rides that making a fuss about being behind other horses just wastes his energy, although some never do manage to settle quietly at the start.

It helps a great deal if the rider can relax his body and communicate his relaxed state to his horse, although this is difficult when you are excited or nervous too and probably anticipating trouble from the horse. There are two theories on coping with the situation. One is that you should let the horse go so that he will use up his uncontrollable freshness without wasting energy fighting you, and will then settle down. There are problems with this approach, however. An inexperienced horse who is unmanageable at the start is likely to resent other horses overtaking him until he is quite tired. Also, an overexcited horse is likely to become unbalanced, careering along at speed and certainly won't be paying much attention to the ground beneath his feet. You therefore run a greater risk of injury from stony or uneven going. Yet another problem with this approach is that although you can give yourself a lot of time in hand by going quickly at the start of a ride, it is surprising how soon this is lost once a horse starts to tire. You will also be prevented from riding the competition the way you want and your options for planning how to make the best of the route will be restricted. Five miles of grassy track are no use if your horse can barely manage a trot, having galloped himself out in the first twenty miles.

The second theory of handling the

situation is to hang back. Some riders at a massed start wait several minutes to let the field get ahead before setting off. Personally I would find this approach to the problem too demoralising. It may be easy enough to catch the tail-end riders, but there is little hope of catching the leaders. Even if your horse starts more quietly, he is likely to want to take off again when he sees the first rider ahead.

If you have done your training well, know your horse and what you are aiming for, the best solution is a compromise. To begin with, start with the field, but stay at the back. Use whatever bit it takes to control the horse and keep him out of the way of other riders, without resorting to an exhausting pulling match. Force yourself to stay calm. In his early endurance rides your horse will not be as hard and fit as seasoned horses, no matter how well you have trained him, and after a while he will begin to succumb to the pressure of trying to keep up with them. Don't worry about his exuberance and pulling. Just concentrate on what you are doing and let him know you want his full attention. You must keep your mind on your riding and communicate with your horse. You can't do this if you are tense. Think of balance and rhythm and persist until you achieve them. When the horse realises that it is easier to co-operate than to fight you, he will start to settle.

Riding for a Placing

Tactical riding for a placing demands considerable experience. You must be flexible and adjust your plans continually to take account of the weather, the ground conditions and how the other horses are doing. This is less of a problem on tougher rides, where the terrain sorts the horses out fairly quickly, although you still want to know who is ahead of you and what their strong and weak points might be.

On easy ground, however, breaking away from the field is more difficult, especially if you are acting as pacemaker and they are sticking to you while your horse does all the work. The Summer Solstice Ride has produced a racing finish for three years in succession; exciting for the spectators, but not really what endurance riding is all about.

Sticking to Your Tactics

On familiar ground you may have a pretty good idea of your horse's speeds at different gaits over varied going. Away at a ride, the situation becomes confused by unfamiliar ground and the presence of other horses, some of which will have similar paces to your horse, while others will be completely different.

It is tempting to 'go with the crowd', but far better to ride your own race. You may find yourself going either faster or slower than you planned, passing up the chance to let your horse drink, or having your rhythm broken by other riders who base their riding purely on the clock, regardless of the going. Part company with them. Depending upon your own ride tactics, leave them behind or let them go on ahead. It can be difficult, as while you move on steadily they will continually want to gallop past you, then slow down so that soon you are overtaking them again. This is something your horse will get used to, however, and those kind of riders will invariably disappear before the end of a long ride, withdrawn, eliminated or just left behind.

Fig 54 Tactical riding is difficult on the Summer Solstice Ride in Sherwood Forest. Val Long, Thea Toomer-Baker and Debbie Boots, still together after 85 miles.

Choosing a Pace

Riding to take account of different terrain is an art in itself. Wherever you are riding you want to make use of the best ground to give your horse the best possible chance, so keep your eyes on the trail ahead. Your well-trained trail horse will also have his eyes on the terrain ahead. Too much galloping is not recommended on endurance rides, although it can be tempting when a long green stretch opens up in front of you, especially if your horse is of like mind. If you know that a slow section comes next, a short gallop won't do any harm, as by now your horse is probably into his rhythm enough to revert to a steady, loping canter after a hundred yards or so of exuberance.

Rhythm

Rhythm in all paces is what counts. A canter can often be less tiring for the horse than a trot, but when he is really working at a ground-eating trot, you may well find your suggestion to canter ignored. Your horse knows what he is doing and doesn't want to break his stride. During early training, it is easy for the horse to breathe in rhythm with his canter – you can feel this and perhaps hear it, if it is accompanied by the 'high blowing' that characterises quality horses. As training progresses, the horse will also learn to breathe in time with his trot and as any runner or hill walker knows, breathing in time with your stride makes covering the ground much easier. There is a theory

Fig 55   Maintaining a rhythm – Anthony Hayward on Riching's Bally Blaze, members of the British team in 1985.

that the different phases of a horse's stride are related to the different phases of respiration, so that when they are working in harmony, his whole body becomes more efficient.

Trot

The trot takes two forms: the basic, balanced, shorter striding trot used for picking the way over rough terrain; and the long, powerfully extended but equally balanced, ground covering stride that comes with practice and is the most familiar pace of the endurance horse. The trot is generally thought to be a tiring pace for the horse, but this latter type of trot covers the ground lightly and at speed and the horse can keep it up for long periods of time. Former European Champion Judy Beaumont calls it 'moon striding', an apt description which conveys its lightness and speed.

Coping with Terrain

On roads and stony tracks, make the most of grass verges – though not carefully mown and tended ones outside people's houses as some thoughtless riders have been known to do! If you do have to ride over loose stones, slow down and keep the horse balanced, so he is less likely to slam his foot down on a sharp stone and get a cut or bruise. The loss of a few minutes is better than elimination for lameness.

Fig 56   Tackling difficult country is what it is all about for riders coming off Pen-y-Gadair, the second highest peak in the Black Mountains.

Moorland and forest tracks, where many British rides are held, usually offer pretty good going, but routes may cross open country where there are few tracks and the ground is uneven. Watch out for holes and unexpected ditches and give your horse his head so he can see where he is going. A fast moving horse on uneven territory will naturally carry his head low. As the rider, you should be looking a little further ahead, ready to help the horse if need be, staying balanced over his centre of motion and interfering as little as possible. In this way your horse can trot or canter over what may seem to you alarmingly rough going, both uphill and down.

Hills

There is a lot said about the inadvisability of trotting downhill, owing to the strain it puts on the horse's legs. However, if you are riding in a competition where there are many hills to cope with, time lost walking down every hill will be difficult to make up on the rest of the course. The key, once again, is balance. Horses brought up and trained on hills soon learn how to cope with them, and if your horse wants to go downhill a little faster than he would go up, why not make the most of it.

If a horse is unused to hills, you might descend more quickly by dismounting and running alongside, freeing his back

Fig 57 Fording the Cryne Fawr on the Red Dragon Ride.

muscles from the effort of carrying you and allowing them to work more effectively. In the United States, 'tailing' is the accepted method of getting up steep hills and giving the horse a break from carrying the rider. This is done by converting your reins to a long lead rope, going behind the horse and letting him help to pull you up, holding on to his tail. Of course, you are supposed to put some effort into the exercise too. It seems to work well, although at one point on the Tevis trail, at a place called Last Chance, I was so busy taking photographs of horses coming up the trail that I failed to notice that one had parted company with his rider until I heard the plaintive shout from down the hill 'Can ya catch ma horse!'

Going up a steep hill, it can be easier to zigzag. Going down, the safest way is to keep straight, as the horse will be less likely to slip.

Ride Hazards

Dangers on rides depend on the country you are in. Outside Britain they may range from excessive heat to snake bites, and in the States we were warned about poison ivy. In Britain, bad weather, bogs and dangerous cliffs are the worst hazards you are likely to meet. If you are competing in one of the tougher rides, find out the safety procedures and take all safety warnings seriously. The first and most important rule is if you get into trouble, *never*, under any circumstances, leave the ride route. Doing so might make it impossible for searchers to find you.

If you stay on the route, you will also avoid dangerous terrain. Never try to take short cuts and never cross rivers except at established fords. Safe river fords will usually have a sandy area at each side, while muddy banks may be unsafe.

Bogs are easy to recognise once you know what to look for – brightly coloured vegetation, such as vivid green grass and mosses or yellow grass and rushes, sometimes with 'bog cotton' growing amongst them. Anything which vividly contrasts with the surrounding safe, brownish-green ground may be a bog. Bogs are frequently found on the tops of hills as well as in valleys, so being on high ground is no guarantee of safety.

Fog is a danger on the moors and if you are on a ride when fog comes down to the extent that you cannot see the way ahead, you should stay exactly where you are until it lifts or help arrives. There may be a terrible temptation to go on and try to find your way out of it, but if you cannot actually see the route markers, you will simply wander in circles, perhaps meeting worse dangers. Stay put and give a shout every so often to help searchers find you.

Veterinary Checkpoints

Your success in the competition will be greatly helped by the efficiency of your crew at the halts. Always aim to come in at a halt slowly, having given your horse a chance to start recovering during the past mile or so.

The first priority should be a drink for both your horse and yourself. This is the time to offer your horse an electrolyte drink. If he accepts it, fine, if not, offer plain water. Your horse should, of course, be allowed to drink from suitable water sources during the ride, but he will probably not take more than a few

mouthfuls. If he drinks more, be careful to regulate your speed for a while, when you set off again.

At a halt, it is up to your crew to do the actual work on the horse; you should take the opportunity to rest and eat. However, you will want to keep an eye on things and discuss with the crew any problems you may have encountered, as well as finding out how the rest of the ride is going.

How the horse is treated will depend on the weather – if it is hot, he will need more cooling out than if it is cold. The first priority is to have him ready to present to the vet at the correct time, in sound condition and with his pulse and respiration rates within the permitted parameters.

For a half-hour halt you will not want to remove the bridle, and will probably leave the saddle on too, having loosened the girth. In any case, it is advisable to leave the saddle on for a while whenever you have a halt, and at the end of the ride, to avoid the risk of pressure bumps. Not all horses are subject to these, but it is worth taking the precaution.

If it is hot, give the horse a quick wash down, starting with his head and neck, then legs, shoulders and belly. The application of water to the skin reduces the need for the horse to sweat to cool his system by evaporation, so reducing the risk of dehydration. In very hot weather, though these conditions seldom occur in Britain, it may be necessary to cool the horse down quickly for vetting. However, as a general rule do not apply cold water to the back and hind quarters, as

cooling down these large muscle masses too fast can cause cramps, with the risk of muscle strain. In cooler weather, simply sponge off enough mud and sweat to make the horse comfortable.

On shorter halts let the horse pick at some hay or grass, but if you have an hour, as you will on the longest rides, take his bridle off and offer him some feed. He may or may not want it. Let him rest during the break, only walking him gently if there is a danger that he might stiffen up.

When tending the horse, check him over straight away as you work, for any lumps, bumps, cuts or grazes and attend to them as appropriate.

Don't let the horse get cold. If there is a breeze, put a light cooler on him as soon as possible and if the wind is cold or the day sharp, a blanket or warm rug. A blanket or cooler that comes all the way up to his ears is better than the conventional British type. An anti-sweat rug should not be used without another rug over it – it will not help the horse dry off, cool down or stay warm.

One of the main attributes of a good crew is their ability to think and adjust their routine to take account of the conditions. Sadly, one still sees shivering horses without rugs, or worse having buckets of cold water poured over them; conversely, one sees tired, possibly dehydrated horses with elevated pulse-rates left standing in the sun when they could have been in the shade of a tree.

Pulse and Respiration Rates

On a hot day, if your horse's pulse or respiration rate is too high to pass the vetting comfortably, you have a maximum of half an hour in which to get it

Fig 58 (Opposite)   *'Can ya catch ma horse!'*

down. In this case, the object is to cool the horse down, running as much cold water over him as possible. Soaked sponges or towels over his poll, neck and withers will help – keep changing them. Water playing as much as possible over the large veins in his neck and inside his legs will speed up his recovery. Massaging the muscles of his shoulders and quarters will help redistribute the blood from them and aid the cooling process.

Keep the horse quiet and let him rest as much as possible. Don't walk him or let him eat – he is unlikely to be interested in food anyway. If his pulse is not down after thirty minutes despite your efforts, and there is nothing else obviously wrong with him, accept the fact that he was just not fit enough to do the ride in the way you had planned and resolve to do something about it before the next competition.

The reasons for a high respiration rate are twofold. It increases the amount of oxygen entering the system to satisfy the oxygen debt due to excessive work and moves air in and out of the lungs in an attempt to extract heat from the body. The second cause is the most likely on long rides in hot weather conditions. By cooling the horse with water we remove the need for him to pant and so reduce the respiratory rate.

Looking after Yourself

While the crew are looking after the horse, the rider should be resting and having something to eat. It is the crew's

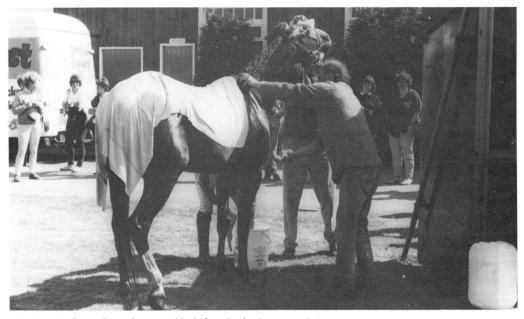

Fig 59   Cooling a horse down quickly before the final vetting of the Summer Solstice Ride – wet towels, plenty of cool water and a small square of shade.

job to keep an eye on the time and make sure you are ready for the vetting and to restart. During a ride, with the adrenalin pumping away, you are unlikely to feel very hungry but it is important that you eat something. Tiredness becomes much more of a problem when your body is in need of nourishment.

Concentrate on energy giving food and have something that you like packed ready for you, whether it is chocolate bars or cheese sandwiches, though the best food is usually the kind that slips down easily – hot soup is energy giving on a cold day, otherwise pure fruit juices are good. Sticky, fizzy drinks will make you thirsty. Some riders carry glucose tablets on the ride, but they are also likely to make you thirsty.

Electrolyte drinks for humans, such as Staminade, are very useful when you get tired during a ride, particularly when your crew meets you at pre-arranged points, but you don't want to stop for more than a few seconds. It doesn't take long for you and your horse to swill down a dose of electrolytes, which at such times taste like nectar from heaven!

While your horse is drinking, your crew will be giving him a quick swill down on a hot day, which helps to prevent dehydration and keeps him fresh on the ride. You will frequently find the remains of the bucket of water thrown over both of you as you depart – it is about the only way the crew can get their own back on a touchy rider who wants everything done yesterday!

Meeting your crew between veterinary checkpoints is very important on

Fig 60   Refreshment for horse and rider – Denise Passant and Ferhanoush.

long rides, as they provide practical help and moral support for both horse and rider when they are getting tired. There is no more welcome sight than that of your husband, daughter, wife, friend or other 'volunteer' standing ready with the buckets as you complete another section of the course.

Bad-tempered riders and long suffering, patient crews are part of endurance riding folklore. When you begin, you may have to explain to your crew that you don't really mean whatever you say about them after ninety miles!

At the end of the ride comes the final vetting, and the way you handle the horse during those vital thirty minutes can mean the difference between success and failure. We will discuss it in more detail in the following chapter.

Post-ride Care

Finally, don't forget your horse once the competition has finished. Make him as comfortable as possible in his stable, or for the journey home, and keep an eye on him in case any problems develop. Where horses remain stabled on the night after a competition, there is always a vet on call. Give your horse a small feed once he has settled down and if he eats up, he can have another several hours later. Fill his hay-net, and once you are sure he is not dehydrated, he can have his usual free access to water.

Let him relax after a ride before you take him home, and when you arrive turn him out if you can. He will unwind more easily outside and will keep moving as he grazes, which will prevent his muscles from stiffening up as they would in a stable. Similarly, if your horse is staying at the ride venue overnight, walk him gently after the ride to help him relax and to prevent stiffness. If possible, walk him where he can graze a little.

After a long ride, your horse can rest for up to a week. On no account give him any hard work. You will learn what suits him best, and whether he will benefit from gentle exercise. In any case, he should be turned out for most of the day. While he is off work, reduce his hard feed and make sure he has some company. You will, of course, be tending to him twice a day as usual, but the odd social visit, with an apple or carrot, will not go unappreciated. By the time you have completed a few endurance rides with your horse, you should have established a fairly strong bond and he should always be pleased to see you.

12 Veterinary Judging

Veterinary judging is part and parcel of the whole philosophy of distance riding, as the object of the sport is to encourage better horsemanship and higher levels of performance without causing distress to the horse. Although the anxiety of waiting for vetting can produce tension and occasionally argument, another object of the sport is that it should be enjoyable; try not to let the disappointment of being 'spun' (failed by the vet), which will happen from time to time, cloud the pleasure of taking part.

On the whole, veterinary surgeons understand the riders' feelings and recognise how much hard work goes into training a horse for a long distance ride. They may not have time to discuss your problems with you there and then – it is hard work vetting forty or fifty horses without a break – but they will almost always be prepared to spare you some time after the ride, or at a less hectic moment. Be patient and realise that they have a job to do.

Preparing for the Vet

Before you compete in your first ride, teach your horse what will be expected of him at the vetting. Ride vets are frequently souls of patience with horses, but when time is pressing, nothing is more annoying than a horse who does not behave. Your horse must stand still to have his pulse and respiration rates taken and to be examined for 'lumps and bumps'. He must consent to having his legs felt and his feet picked up and examined. Finally, he must trot out freely in hand when asked to do so. He must do all this in a competition environment with other horses milling round and waiting in line and he must accept their presence with equanimity.

The Pre-ride Vetting

When you arrive for the pre-ride vetting you should present your horse in a clean and tidy condition, tacked according to the rules. BHS LDR Group rules stipulate that the horse must be presented in a bridle, presumably to give the handler better control if necessary. EHPS rules require a headcollar, on the basis that the horse ought to be sufficiently well behaved to be presented in a headcollar, and this makes examination of the mouth easier.

No other tack may be worn and if you intend to use bandages or boots on the ride, they must be left off until after the vetting. Rugs may remain in place until you are called, but don't delay the proceedings while you take them off. Feet must be picked out but must not be oiled, as the vet will examine them and he does not want to have to pick up 200 oiled feet!

On BHS rides, the organiser will have filled in your vet card with information provided on your entry form, but you must declare any problems, such as current minor injuries, gait abnormalities or other defects.

For EHPS rides your vet sheet will be sent to you with your ride information and you must fill it in, take it with you to the ride and hand it in to the vet. Again, any lesions or defects must be declared on the form.

For most rides you will be given a specific time for vetting, usually about half an hour before the start, but the previous day for major rides. Be on time. Lateness means penalty points in EHPS rides and, in any ride, the organiser will not thank you for upsetting the arrangements.

The purpose of pre-ride vetting is to establish base parameters for pulse, respiration and dehydration, and to assess the general condition of the horse, as well as to decide whether he may be allowed to start the competition.

Pulse and Respiration

CTRs use the base pulse-rate as one of the criteria for awarding gradings. Normal pulse-rate is reckoned to lie between 36 and 42 beats per minute. If the actual pulse-rate is below or above these limits, then either 36 or 42 respectively will be taken as the base rate in CTRs. The recovery rate after the ride is then judged by its closeness to the base rate.

On all EHPS rides, the maximum pulse-rate allowed for a horse to pass the veterinary judging is 60 beats per minute, and the maximum respiration rate, 48 beats per minute. If the respiration rate exceeds the pulse-rate, the horse is eliminated.

On BHS LDR Group rides, the maximum permitted parameters are a pulse-rate of 64 and a respiration rate of 36. On some major rides, penalties are awarded

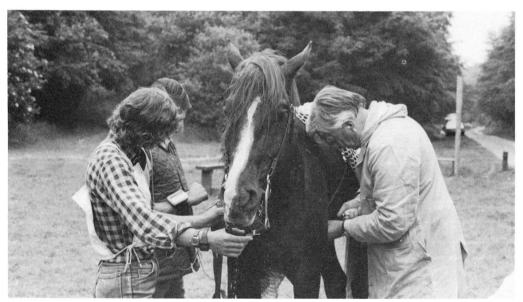

Fig 61   Checking the pulse at a mandatory halt.

for pulse-rates in excess of 56 beats per minute at the end of the day's ride.

The validity of respiration rates in assessing a horse's condition is doubtful, and there is an argument that these should be used as a check to confirm other signs of distress, rather than as a final arbiter. A horse suffering from oxygen debt may well gasp and breathe heavily, but a perfectly fit, yet hot, horse may well pant shallowly to aid cooling, without being in any way distressed. Genuinely high respiration, signifying distress, is usually accompanied by a high heart rate and possibly other problems.

Dehydration

Dehydration can be a serious problem in hot conditions, so it is important to get some idea of a horse's normal state of dehydration at the start of the ride. This is usually done by means of the 'pinch test', whereby a fold of skin at the base of the neck is pinched out between finger and thumb and the number of seconds (from one to five) that it takes to return to normal is recorded. For this test to have any value, it must be done by the same veterinary surgeon at each check, and at the same place on the neck.

Dehydration is rarely a problem on British rides, unless a sudden heatwave occurs, when horses may have to cope with hot conditions to which they are not accustomed. Using plenty of water on the horse's head, neck, chest and legs during the ride will help prevent dehydration, as it reduces the need to sweat. Dehydrated horses should be offered small amounts of water, at frequent intervals, until they have recovered. Seriously dehydrated horses may be subject to colic attacks and require veterinary attention

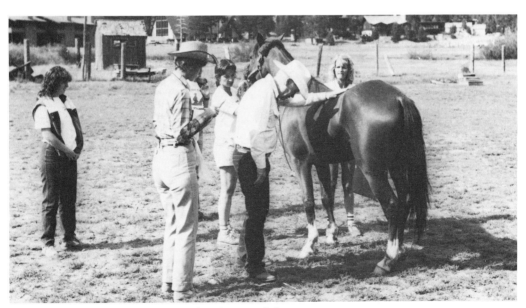

Fig 62   Taking respiration base rate before the start of the Tevis Cup Ride.

to replace the body fluids as quickly as possible.

Other Checks

The mucous membranes of the eyes and mouth are examined. When normal they are salmon pink in colour, but become darker and reddened when a horse becomes seriously stressed. A note may be made of the capillary refill rate of the gums, which is tested by exerting firm thumb pressure at a spot above the teeth. The normal rate of one to three seconds may slow down when a horse becomes overstressed.

Your horse will also be checked over for 'lumps and bumps', any swellings, mouth sores, wounds, brushing marks, girth galls, saddle sores or marks, and any tender areas or other defects which might become worse on the ride. Old lesions will be ignored, but any current problems which may seriously worsen could mean that the horse will be refused permission to start.

Trotting Up

Finally, your horse's feet and legs will be examined and he will be trotted up for soundness. You may be asked to walk away and trot back, or to trot in both directions. Alternatively, you may be asked to trot in a figure of eight, as is increasingly the practice for major rides. It is worth spending some time teaching your horse to trot out well, otherwise

Fig 63 Gary Cook inspects Pam James' mount, Packman, during the 1985 Tevis Cup Ride. British vet Rod Fisher, acting as Pam's back-up, looks on.

you will continually find yourself being asked to run up twice, or even three times. You should hold the lead rope at least a foot from the horse's head so that his head and neck are free and he can move straight. The vet wants to see the horse, not the rider, which he cannot do if the rider is obscuring his view while hanging on to the horse's head.

Ensure that your horse trots out smartly – dragging feet invariably lead to a repeat performance being required. When you reach the point to turn, slow down and turn at a walk – the vet doesn't want to see your horse fall over! Always turn to the right, so that you do not put yourself between the horse and the vet. Trot back straight towards the vet, but try to slow down as you reach him and not run him down!

When your horse is trotted up, the vet will note any peculiarities of gait, so that they are not mistaken for lameness later in the ride, when a different vet may be on duty.

Your horse's feet and shoes will be examined. It is as well to have your horse shod about a week before a ride, so that the shoes are in good condition to cope with the mileage but have had time to bed down. The vet may refer you to the farrier if there is anything he is not satisfied with, but on many rides it will not be possible to have reshoeing done at the start.

As far as possible the same vet will examine your horse for the same points throughout the ride. It is not unusual at a major ride for your horse to be examined by three different vets – one doing pulse and respiration rates, one on 'lumps and bumps' and a third checking feet and trotting up.

Veterinary Checkpoints

During the ride, various forms of veterinary checkpoints may be used. On a 100-mile ride, for example, it is usual to have four checks during the ride, in addition to the pre- and post-ride vetting. These would normally be a 30 minute halt and check at 25 miles, an hour halt at 50 miles, another 30 minute at 75 miles and a spot check with a maximum 15 minute hold for pulse and respiration rates at 90 miles.

Alternatively a system of veterinary gates may be used, whereby it is the rider's responsibility to check that his horse's pulse and respiration rates are down sufficiently before presenting him to the vet. If they are found to be too high, they may be rechecked at 10 minute intervals until the horse is passed to continue on the ride. The maximum time a rider can remain at a gate, before being eliminated, is 30 minutes.

No time allowance is made for stopping at veterinary gates, so ideally you should arrive with your horse's pulse and respiration rates within the permitted parameters so that you can continue straight away. To know how far before the checkpoint you need to slow down is a skill which requires practice. A second art required in gated rides is knowing when your horse is ready to be presented. It is better to wait an extra two or three minutes before presenting him, than to be held for ten minutes because his rates are too high.

The extent of the veterinary inspection at mandatory halts may vary. LDR Group rules tend to be formally enforced, and the horse should be presented without the saddle and in a bridle. If conditions are muddy, it helps if an attempt has been made to clean the horse

Fig 64   Exchanging notes – British vet Tony Pavord (right), chatting to Gary Cook DVM, from Montana during the Tevis Cup Ride.

Fig 65   Scene of the final vetting at Exford. Jackie Taylor trots up Beltane Phoenix for vet Alec McGuiness.

up. You may not be required to remove the saddle for half-hour halts. Having passed the checks on pulse and respiration rates, you may simply be asked to trot up mounted as you leave the checkpoint, particularly on endurance rides.

The third type of check you might encounter is the spot check, which may be made at any time and for which no time allowance is given. These are usually done if for some reason the veterinary surgeons want to keep an eye on a particular horse which is causing them concern, but which has not yet actually reached the point of being eliminated. Spot checks are therefore simply a further means of safeguarding the welfare of the horse.

The Final Inspection

The most nerve-racking veterinary inspection is that which takes place at the end of the ride. You have completed the course, but your horse may not pass the final hurdle. If you were not so busy attending to your horse, that half-hour wait could seem like hours!

The final vetting takes a similar form to the pre-ride vetting and the most common causes of elimination are lameness and pulse-rates above the set parameters.

Lameness during rides is usually the result of stone bruises and, in the hind limbs, muscle damage. Stone bruises are an unfortunate fact of life. Covering so many miles, your horse is bound to step on a sharply protruding stone and run up lame at some point, however carefully you ride. Muscle damage may be caused directly by fatigue – tired muscles unable to meet the demand for sustained effort, lose their elasticity and succumb to a pull

or strain. Serious muscle fatigue may lead to extensive muscle fibre damage, the symptoms of which are very similar to azoturia or tying up. Unless urgent veterinary attention is sought, death due to kidney failure may result.

Elevated pulse-rates may occur if the horse was not fit enough for the ride and his heart is trying to cope with the excessive stress imposed. There may be another cause; for example, a lame or dehydrated horse will often have an elevated pulse. At the vetting the elevated pulse may be the only sign of a problem, the cause not becoming apparent until later.

An elevated respiration rate sometimes leads to elimination and it may be accompanied by the development of 'thumps', an irregular spasm of the diaphragm. The exact cause of this condition is not known, but it seems to be the equine equivalent of a bad case of hiccups.

On some rides, such as EHPS CTRs, the Golden Horseshoe Ride and the Goodwood 100, penalties may be awarded for minor injuries, and for pulse and respiration rates outside the optimum.

After the Ride

It is after the final vetting and during the hours following the ride that questions start to be asked about why things went wrong. If you are eliminated in a ride, it is always for a valid reason, so turn the experience into a constructive one: work out what went wrong, where and why, and do something about it so that it doesn't happen next time. Occasionally the reason may be purely bad luck or, still more rarely, a horse who simply isn't cut out for long distance riding, but the problem nearly always boils down to

Fig 66   After the ride the vet will invariably be prepared to give help and advice.

something that could have been avoided with more knowledge and a better training programme.

It is very important to keep an eye on your horse after a ride, and all the more important if he has been eliminated. A horse who came in with a high pulse or slightly lame behind might tie up, develop colic due to dehydration or exhaustion, or show other signs of illness. A horse who becomes seriously ill should not be expected to travel, and if you have any doubts about the well-being of your horse, call in a vet.

Vetting on international rides may take place some hours after the ride, and sometimes not until the following day, giving ample time for any problems to manifest themselves. Such rides have been won and lost on the owners' ability to care for their horses and to bring them out sound for vetting after such a lapse of time.

It is particularly important to cool the horse out thoroughly at the end of the ride, walking him to alleviate stiffness and doing everything possible to see that he is able to relax. He can be allowed to graze a little whilst walking, but should not be fed for about two hours, by which time his bodily systems should have returned to normal and should be able to cope with digesting some food. However, only a light feed should be given at this stage. It is claimed that massaging the muscles of the neck, quarters, shoulders and thighs prevents horses from stiffening up for the following day.

If you reach the second or third day of a ride, do not expect your horse to come straight out of the stable in the morning and pass the vet. Walk him, or lunge him a little, to loosen him up first. Simple, passive stretching exercises, pulling the horse's legs gently forwards, backwards and to the side before starting work are also said to be beneficial.

13 Major Rides

Britain now has a growing number of major long distance and endurance rides in various parts of the country. Some are also designated ELDRIC Trophy rides and one, the Goodwood 100, is run under FEI (Federation Equestre Internationale) rules.

Golden Horseshoe Ride

This is the oldest and best known of Britain's long distance rides. It was first run in 1965 and since 1974 has been based at the village of Exford, on Exmoor, Somerset. It is organised by the BHS LDR Group and is the only LDR Group ride for which the horses have to be qualified. The reason for this is that it is run early in the season, in mid-May, and it is felt that some proof of fitness is required. The Golden Horseshoe is a gold series ride, so riders must also have qualified under the rider qualification system introduced in 1985. The qualifying rides for horses take the form of 40-mile rides which must be completed at 7.5 m.p.h. and horses must pass the vetting.

The final is a 100-mile ride, run over two days, and it is a medal ride, with gold medals going to those who successfully complete the distance at an average speed on each day of not less than 8 m.p.h. It is not a race. Silver and bronze medals, and completion rosettes are awarded on the basis of speed and veterinary penalty points.

Conditions on the Golden Horseshoe Ride can vary enormously from year to year. As it is early in the season the weather can range from snow to temperatures above 80 degrees Fahrenheit, and both extremes have been known. The going can be good and dry, or extremely heavy. The route itself is changed every year and offers many different challenges – fair, springy turf; rough, stony tracks; short, sharp ascents and descents; and long, daunting pulls. There is open moorland, wooded coombes, where humidity can be a problem in hot years, and the minimum of roadwork.

The changing conditions have produced wildly fluctuating results. For example, in 1985, when the ride was still run over 75 miles, 34 gold medals were awarded. In 1986, the first 100-mile year, no one achieved a gold medal. In 1979, a year of extremely bad weather conditions, the lone gold went to Mary Towneley's Miss Muffett, a very successful long distance horse, who has five gold awards from the Golden Horseshoe Ride to her credit.

The advent of rider qualifications reduced the number of entries for the 1986 ride, but it is still the best supported ride of any on the LDR Group calendar, offering as it does the unique challenge of some of Britain's toughest and most beautiful country combined with an established tradition as the Group's premier ride.

*Fig 67   Sally Scorey comes in at the half-way halt on the Golden
Horseshoe Ride.*

Fig 68   Margaret Montgomerie riding Tarquin.

Summer Solstice Ride

This is the British Open Endurance Riding Championship. Run by the EHPS, it was Britain's first established one-day, 100-mile ride. It was established in 1978 and for several years it was run in Sussex, on the South Downs, until it was moved to Sherwood Forest in Nottinghamshire. This is a true endurance ride and although the number of entries has yet to exceed twenty, competition is extremely fierce for placings.

The going in the Forest is, for the most part, good – long, level tracks where speed can be maintained. This produces a difficult tactical dilemma, as the leading riders have little opportunity to make the break from each other during the ride, and for three years running the Summer Solstice has produced a racing finish. In 1985 this resulted in both horses concerned being eliminated with high pulse-rates, although both were produced fit and sound the next day. Valerie Long, who won the ride in 1984, was one of the two eliminated in 1985 and won again in 1986, all with her Arab stallion, Tarim. He is the current record holder, with an average speed for the 100 miles of 10.2 m.p.h. and a riding time of 9 hours 49 minutes.

The atmosphere at the Summer Solstice Ride typifies all that is best in endurance riding: tremendous support for the riders and a long day that begins at 2.30 a.m., trotting up horses under the racecourse lighting at Southwell; the start, with the way lit for the riders by motorbikes from the Trail Riders Fellowship; the ride itself, with crews hurrying to keep up with their riders, all willing to give a helping hand to someone else if need be; the frequently emotional finish, and the tense wait for the final vetting, then the cheers as the results are announced. By the time the last rider crosses the line, most of the excitement is over, but however late this may be, there is always someone to applaud the latecomer over the finish. As an example of the comradeship found in the sport, in 1986 Margaret Montgomerie took the redoubtable Tarquin out on the trail after dark, to meet a solitary last competitor who was walking in, and rode with her for those last long, lonely miles.

The Goodwood International 100-mile Ride

This ride, run by the LDR Group, is a two-day endurance ride of 100 miles, with 50 miles covered on each day. The winner is the rider with the fastest time overall, after any veterinary penalties have been added. The ride is run under FEI rules and is also used as the basis of selection for team riders to represent Britain in international championships.

The route is over the South Downs in Sussex and really is a test of stamina and endurance as the ride takes the form of a 'gated' ride. This means that instead of a mandatory wait at veterinary checkpoints, riders arrive at the halt and may present their horses at the veterinary gate as soon as they think their pulse and respiration rates are down to the permitted parameters. This calls for more skill on the rider's part, as the ideal, to maintain speed, is to arrive at the checkpoint with pulse and respiration rates low enough to go straight out again. No time allowance is given for halts on 'gated' rides, and if a horse is not fit to continue within thirty minutes of entering the gate, he is eliminated.

The terrain at Goodwood is fair, open and includes some steep hills, the main hazard being sharp flints on the tracks.

Black Mountains Ride

Considered by many to be the toughest British long distance ride, this three-day LDR Group ride takes place amid some of the country's most spectacular mountain scenery in South Wales. It is a medal ride, run on the same basis as the Golden Horseshoe Ride, with a gold speed of 8 m.p.h. The route comprises mainly mountain tracks with some forestry and some extremely steep hills. The going is mainly good, the ride being held in September, although rain can result in some areas being wet and heavy.

The distance is 110 miles which in different years has been split in different ways – 40/40/30 in 1984, 50/30/30 in 1985 and 30/50/30 in 1986. This ride really tests the ability of horses to cope with difficult terrain and come out fit and sound three days in succession.

As with most rides, shorter distance classes are run in conjunction with the main event, and because of the way the main class is organised, the Black Mountains Ride provides a particularly wide choice, from 80 miles down to 15 miles. If 110 miles is too daunting, it is well worth entering one of the shorter classes, purely for the experience of riding in the mountains.

Fig 69   Belinda Brigg on Reproach tackles the Black Mountains.

National Championship

This ride has grown out of the 80-mile Three Rivers Ride at Salisbury, run for the first time in 1985. It is a one-day, 100-mile ride, organised by the LDR Group and has been designated the sport's National Championship. It is an endurance ride and is also a 'gated' ride, which makes it the first 100-mile 'gated' ride to be run in Great Britain. It took place for the first time at the end of August 1986.

Cotswold 100

The first LDR Group one-day, 100-mile ride took place at the end of May 1986 from Cheltenham racecourse, over a route described as testing, but fair. Eight horses started the ride and six finished. The winner, by a short head, was Jackie Taylor on Beltane Phoenix, from Gill Shutt on Triella, with Carole Tuggey on El Askar a length away in third place. The winning speed was 7.39 m.p.h., in a riding time of 13 hours 32 minutes, considerably slower than the Summer Solstice record, but on more taxing ground.

Red Dragon Ride

This ELDRIC Trophy ride, run by the EHPS, moved in 1985 from mid-Wales to the Black Mountains, and is now run

Fig 70   Waiting to start at the Red Dragon Ride.

over much the same route as the Black Mountains Ride. It is, however, an endurance ride of 100 miles over two days and presents an alternative challenge to its three-day counterpart. In its first year at its new home there were no completions, although this was partly due to route markers being removed and riders getting lost. It is undoubtedly the toughest ride on the EHPS calendar and one of the biggest challenges in British distance riding today.

Breamore

The third ELDRIC Trophy ride run by the EHPS is a 50-mile endurance ride in the New Forest. The going is extremely fast and the record is held by Charlotte Beard on Cariad, who completed the 1985 ride in 3 hours 33 minutes, a speed of just over 14 m.p.h. This was an exceptional effort. In 1986 the ride was won by Lesley Dunn on Bonanza, at the more realistic speed of 12.7 m.p.h.

ELDRIC Trophy

The Trophy is awarded for the European Points Championship, instigated in 1980. Riders must compete in not more than four designated Trophy rides in at least two countries. Points are awarded according to placings irrespective of whether a rider intends to compete for the Trophy, and comparatively more points are gained for a placing in a one-day ride than in a ride of two or more days.

Fig 71 'Potato' Richardson (centre) from California, who has completed many Tevis Cup Rides, stops to speak to a friend at Michigan Bluff.

Summary

By the time you are thinking about entering for some of these rides, you will have become well and truly 'hooked' on the sport. Along the way, you will have learned a great deal about horses, both riding and horse care, and about your own ability to rise to a challenge. You will have experienced the 'high' that a successful completion or placing brings and will know how to grit your teeth and cope with defeat. You will have made new and lasting friendships and learned the meaning of the true sportsmanship and comradeship that exists among distance riders everywhere.

You may compete abroad, in some of the European rides, or perhaps even in the ultimate endurance challenges, the Australian Quilty Ride or the American Tevis Cup. The Quilty takes place in the steep Blue Mountains of New South Wales and attracts riders from all over the world. The Tevis, still rated the toughest ride in the world, follows the old Pony Express trails over the Sierra Nevada in California. Wendell T. Robie first rode the Tevis trail, to prove that modern horses could still do what the pioneers' horses of the previous century did, and one of the primary aims of the Tevis has always been to seek ever higher standards of horsemanship. Remember this wherever your distance riding career takes you. Winning is fine, but riding is what it is all about.

Fig 72   Pam James collecting her Tevis Buckle at the awards ceremony at Auburn, California, 1985.

Appendix   Organising a Ride

Long distance rides in Britain are organised by volunteers, usually under the auspices of one of the two societies involved, the EHPS and the BHS LDR Group. Volunteer organisers are always welcome to put more rides on the calendar.

Guidelines

Anyone contemplating organising a ride, however, should realise that it does require a considerable amount of time and energy to do a good job. Here are some guidelines on what is required.

The Ride Committee

Before you do anything else, establish who you can rely upon to help. Offers of assistance made when the project is first enthusiastically discussed often disappear when the time comes for real practical help. Be sure you have helpers who are as keen as you are and set up a small committee, with each member having responsibility for a particular aspect of the ride. The main aspects to be sorted out are finance, administration (organising the paperwork and making sure the rules are complied with), route planning and marking, and vetting.

Finance

This is a difficult problem, especially if you are starting up a new ride. If you are organising a ride for one of the main societies, find out how much help you can expect from them. For example, the BHS LDR Group will provide the record cards and paperwork, plus some awards and, most importantly, public liability insurance. However, an affiliation fee must be paid, plus capitation fees for each entry.

Sponsorship is actively sought by many ride organisers and some seem to be more successful in obtaining this very valuable financial support than others. Potential sponsors need to be approached well in advance, preferably the previous year, so that they can plan their budgets accordingly. Even small amounts of money can make the difference between a ride being financially successful, or making a loss.

The level at which you set your entry fees will also make a difference to the financial viability of the ride. These may be laid down by society rules, or you may be able to fix your own level of fees. If the latter, work out the likely expenses of the ride and the likely number of entries (a calculated guess for your first ride) to find how much each will have to pay to cover the cost. This is the minimum you can afford to charge without making a loss.

If you can find an enthusiastic person with some financial or accounting knowledge to take responsibility for this aspect of the ride, it will make the task much easier.

Rules

Each organisation has its own rules and it is important that you are aware of these and run your ride in accordance with them. Non-compliance with the rules may invalidate your insurance cover. The rules will also cover what classes can be run and how they are judged.

If you are running an independent ride, make sure that you take out any necessary insurance cover and include a disclaimer of liability in your ride information to competitors.

The Route

Planning a suitable route is one of the most difficult aspects of ride organisation. It must be suitable to be ridden, so have it planned by a rider and try it out on horseback before committing yourself to it. This may sound like stating the obvious, but there are places where walkers may go which are impassable to riders, and other places where riders may conflict with cyclists or walkers.

Care must be taken not to offend other path users and all necessary permissions to cross privately owned land must be sought well in advance. The laws regarding access, even to common land, are not as simple as they might seem, and the person responsible for planning the route should make sure that everyone involved is contacted. There may be two people to contact regarding one piece of land, for example a landlord and a tenant. National Parks, the National Trust, the Forestry Commission and other statutory bodies may all have a say in the matter. Of course, statutory bridleways may be used, but it is at least courteous to inform the owners of land where bridleways

exist that an organised event will be taking place, that markers will be put out before the ride and that they will be removed immediately afterwards.

In planning the route itself, distances must be worked out very carefully, preferably on the ground. As this is not always possible, they may be taken from a large-scale map, using a map measurer. An extra mile or two will make a difference to the time allowed to complete at a specified speed.

A suitable means of marking the route must be found. On open country flags are best, while in wooded country and on well-defined paths, fluorescent tape works well and can be attached to gateposts, trees or hedges. Orange seems to be the most easily visible colour. Be particularly careful marking areas where the route crosses itself, or is ridden in both directions, so that riders do not get confused.

How often markers should appear is another question. On very open country without defined paths, markers should obviously be in line of sight, one marker being clearly visible from the next. However, where the route is obviously well defined, fewer markers are needed. Mark at junctions and wherever another path joins the track, and put a second marker shortly after each turning for reassurance.

Schedules and Entry Forms

You may have official entry forms or you may have to devise your own. Your ride schedule should include the following information: classes available; secretary's name, address and telephone number; details of awards and entry fees; declarations; closing date for entries; ride rules regarding veterinary inspections and tack and equipment; details of stabling and accommodation, and of facilities at the ride; a disclaimer of liability and a reservation of the right to cancel the ride or make other alterations as necessary.

The entry form should include all the information necessary to show that the horse and rider are eligible to enter the class, and also the competitor's name, address and telephone number and details of the horse.

People will frequently ask if they can enter after the closing date. You will have to take a decision on this according to how well your classes are filled and the disturbance to your organisation. Whatever you decide, be firm and be consistent. Don't accept one entry and refuse another!

Ride Information

As early as possible before the ride, probably about one week ahead, send out your ride information to competitors. This will include a route map and description of the route (the latter is often omitted, but should be included if possible), details of checkpoints, a list of officials and services, details of the competitor's number, vetting time and start time, directions to the venue and any additional information.

Organisation on the Day

This involves the co-operation of a fairly large number of people, whose assistance you will have to enlist well in advance. They will include a secretary of the day, chief veterinary surgeon, assistants and 'writers', official timekeepers, checkpoint stewards (it is a great help if these can be in radio contact with each other and the base – local citizen's band radio clubs are often delighted to help) and a site steward to organise parking. You may also have an official steward from your main organisation (to deal with any disputes or other problems), a tack inspector, farrier (if possible) and your course steward, possibly with helpers.

You must arrange emergency first-aid cover for humans, plus emergency transport and treatment for horses. Before the ride you must inform the local police of the event and put up any warning signs which they might require.

After the Ride

It is not usual to hold award ceremonies after one-day rides as competitors are anxious to get their horses home. Riders may usually collect their awards upon return of their number, after you have had a chance to work out the results.

After the ride, make up your accounts, pay your bills and send thank you letters to everyone who has helped – perhaps they will do the same again next year!

Useful Addresses

Europe and Australia

BHS LDR Group
British Equestrian Centre
Stoneleigh
Kenilworth
Warwickshire CV8 2LR

ELDRIC
Mrs P. Dauster (Secretary)
Pfarrstrasse 7
D-6272 Niedernhausen
West Germany

EHPS of Great Britain
Mr O. Hare (Membership Secretary)
Mill House
Mill Lane
Stoke Bruerne
Northamptonshire NN12 7SH

Australian Endurance Riding
   Association
Pauline Harris
PO Box 235
Gawler
South Australia

USA General Interest

American Horse Council
1700 K Street, N.W., Suite 300
Washington D.C. 20006

National 4-H Council
7100 Connecticut Avenue
Chevy Chase, MD 20815

Horsemanship Safety Association
5304 Reeve Road
Mazomanie, WI 53560

United States Pony Clubs
329 South High Street
West Chester, PA 19382

USA Show and Sport Organisations

American Grandprix Association
Valley Forge Military Academy
   & Junior College
Wayne, PA 19087

American Horse Shows Association
220 East 42nd Street/4th Floor
New York, NY 10017

National Horse Show Association of America
35 Sutton Place
New York, NY 10022

United Professional Horsemen's Association
181 North Mill Street
Lexington, KY 40507

Professional Horsemen's Association of America
S. Lake Street, RR 2, Box 93
Litchfield, CT 06776

United States Combined Training Association
292 Bridge Street
South Hamilton, MA 01982

Further Reading

Black's Veterinary Dictionary, 15th edn (A and C Black Limited 1985).

Houghton Brown, J. and Powell-Smith, V., *Horse and Stable Management* (Granada Publishing 1984).

Hyland, A., *A Guide To Endurance Riding* (The Endurance Horse and Pony Society of Great Britain 1984).

Meade, R., *Fit For Riding* (Batsford 1984).

Rees, L., *The Horse's Mind* (Stanley Paul 1984).

Rose, M., *The Horseman's Notebook* (Harrap Limited 1977).

Swift, S., *Centred Riding* (William Heinemann Limited 1985).

Tellington, W. and Tellington-Jones, L., *Endurance and Competitive Trail Riding* (Doubleday and Company Inc. 1979).

Index

INDEX

Other titles available from The Crowood Press

The Athletic Horse – His Selection,
   Work and Management   *Carol Foster*

Dressage – An Approach to Competition   *Kate Hamilton*

The Equine Veterinary Manual   *Tony Pavord/Rod Fisher*

Show Jumping   *John Smart*

798.23   Drummond, Marcy.
DRU
          Long distance
          riding.

          9-19

$18.95

DATE			